Reviel Netz is Professor of Ar
University, a leading authority or
the Archimedes Palimpsest.

William Noel is Curator of Manuscripts and Rare Books at the Walters Art Museum and Director of the Archimedes Palimpsest Project.

www.archimedespalimpsest.org

THE ARCHIMEDES CODEX

REVEALING THE SECRETS OF THE WORLD'S GREATEST PALIMPSEST

REVIEL NETZ AND
WILLIAM NOEL

PHOENIX

A PHOENIX PAPERBACK

First published in Great Britain in 2007
by Weidenfeld & Nicolson
This paperback edition published in 2008
by Phoenix,
an imprint of Orion Books Ltd,
Orion House, 5 Upper St Martin's Lane,
London WC2H 9EA

An Hachette Livre UK company

1 3 5 7 9 10 8 6 4 2

A CIP catalogue record for this book
is available from the British Library.

ISBN 978-0-7538-2372-9

Typeset by Input Data Services Ltd, Frome

Printed in Great Britain by Mackays of Chatham, plc
Chatham, Kent

CONTENTS

LIST OF ILLUSTRATIONS

This book is dedicated
to Lynn, to Maya, to Darya and Tamara,
and to Ioannes Myronas

PREFACE

Nicetas Choniates, the brother of the Archbishop of Athens, was on the spot to witness the greatest calamity that ever befell the world of learning. In April 1204, Christian soldiers on a mission to liberate Jerusalem stopped short of their goal and sacked Constantinople, the richest city in Europe. Nicetas gave an eyewitness account of the carnage. The sumptuous treasure of the great church of Hagia Sophia (Holy Wisdom) was broken into bits and distributed among the soldiers. Mules were led to the very sanctuary of the church to bear the loot away. A harlot, a worker of incantations and poisonings, sat in the seat of the Patriarch, on which she danced and sang an obscene song. The soldiers captured and raped the nuns that were consecrated to God. 'Oh, immortal God,' cried Nicetas, 'how great were the afflictions of the men.' The obscene realities of medieval warfare crashed upon Constantinople, and the hub of a great empire was shattered.

The looted city had many more books than it had people. This was the first time that Constantinople had been sacked in the 874 years since it was founded by Constantine the Great, Emperor of Rome, in AD 330. Its inhabitants still considered themselves to be Romans and the city held the literary treasures of the ancient world as its inheritance. Among these treasures were treatises by the greatest mathematician of the ancient world and one of the greatest thinkers who had ever lived. He approximated the value of pi, he developed the theory of centres of gravity, and he made steps towards the development of the calculus 1,800 years before Newton and Leibniz.

His name was Archimedes. Unlike hundreds of thousands of books which were destroyed in the sacking of the city, three books containing Archimedes' texts survived.

Of these three books the first to disappear was Codex B; it was last heard of in the Pope's library in Viterbo, north of Rome, in 1311. Next to go was Codex A; it was last recorded in the library of an Italian humanist in 1564. It was through copies of these books that Renaissance masters such as Leonardo da Vinci and Galileo knew the works of Archimedes. But Leonardo, Galileo, Newton and Leibniz knew nothing about the third book. It contained two extraordinary texts by Archimedes that were not in Codices A and B. Next to texts such as these, Leonardo's mathematics looks like child's play. Eight hundred years after the sack of Constantinople this third book, the Archimedes Codex, technically known as Codex C, walked on stage.

This is the true and remarkable story of the book and the texts it contains. It reveals how these texts survived the centuries, how they were discovered, how they disappeared again, and how, eventually, they found a champion. This is also the story of the patient conservation, cutting-edge technology and dedicated scholarship that brought the erased texts back to light. When they started, in 1999, the members of the team that worked on the book had little idea of what they would uncover. By the time they had finished, they had discovered completely new texts from the ancient world and had changed the history of science.

I

Archimedes in America

Archimedes for Sale

NEW YORK, NEW YORK

Felix de Marez Oyens. What a great name! I don't know him, but I saw him on TV once. His name and demeanour together seemed tailor-made to suggest a distinguished and international pedigree, a pedigree that quite naturally produced deep learning, refined taste, excellent judgement and total integrity. He clearly had vast knowledge about books, and he was extraordinarily good at selling them. That's why he was the international director of the Books and Manuscripts Department for Christie's auction house in New York.

Thursday, 29 October 1998 was an exceptionally busy day for Felix. Most of it was devoted to the auction of the final part of the phenomenal collection of books of science and medicine from the collection of Haskell F. Norman. Among the 501 lots were some treasures. In the morning he sold Marie Curie's doctoral thesis, which she had signed for Ernest Rutherford, the man who discovered the nuclear structure of the atom; a first edition of Darwin's *On the Origin of Species*; and a copy of Einstein's 1905 publication on Special Relativity. In the afternoon further extraordinary books were under the hammer: the copy of the first edition of James Clerk Maxwell's *Treatise on Electricity and Magnetism* that had been won as a prize by the man who discovered the electron, J. J. Thompson; Wilbur Wright's first published account of the trial flights at Kitty Hawk, North Carolina; and Nicolai Lobachevskii's *On the Principles of*

Geometry, the first published work on non-Euclidian geometry. Great books, all of them, and a great day for Felix.

Sandwiched between the morning and afternoon sessions of the Norman sale was a separate mini-auction, devoted to one book. It was not a printed book but a handwritten one, and it had not belonged to Norman. In fact, the impressive catalogue that Felix had prepared for the occasion, with the splendid sale code 'Eureka – 9058', doesn't record to whom it did belong. It didn't look like a great book. It was charred by fire, devoured by mould, and it was almost illegible. To make matters worse, just the day before, the Greek Orthodox Patriarchate of Jerusalem had sought a restraining order on Christie's in the US District Court, Southern District of New York, Judge Kimba Wood presiding. The patriarchate argued that the manuscript had been stolen from one of its libraries. Christie's successfully defended their right to auction the book the next day, but it was clear that the case of the rightful ownership of the book would be pursued after the sale. Even with the smart catalogue, the book itself was going to be a hard sell. Who would want an illegible manuscript in appalling condition, and with an ongoing court case attached to it? Nonetheless, at 2 p.m. on this day Felix was determined to sell it for an astronomical sum, and he set the reserve price for the manuscript at $800,000.

Felix hoped that the book would be worth so much because, barely visible underneath thirteenth-century Christian prayers, were the erased words of an ancient legend and a mathematical genius: Archimedes of Syracuse. Incomplete, damaged and overwritten as it was, this book was the earliest Archimedes manuscript in existence. It was the only one that contained *Floating Bodies* – perhaps his most famous treatise – in the original Greek, and the only one that contained any version of two other extraordinary texts – the revolutionary *Method* and the playful *Stomachion*. You can barely read them now but, as Felix was very quick to point out, there was the possibility that the most modern imaging techniques might help. There were other erased texts in the book too, but they were almost invisible; no one could read them and no one had given them much thought. What mattered was that this book contained the extremely battered material remains of the mind of a very great man. If this was a big day for Felix, it was a huge one for the history of science.

The auction room was in Christie's offices on the corner of Park Avenue and 59th Street in New York. The room was lined by large contemporary paintings, which provided the splendid visual setting that the manuscript could not. The manuscript itself was strapped to a book cradle and secured inside a dramatically lit cage to the right of the auctioneer's podium. Reporters arrived as the minutes before the sale were counted down. They stood at the back of the room with their cameramen, who trained their lenses on the book and tried in vain to make it look as photogenic as one of the paintings. The rows furthest from the podium were full. But they were mainly filled with academics, people like the Professor of Mathematics at West Point, Fred Rickey, who was passionate about the manuscript and deeply interested in its fate, but who could not possibly afford it. The seats at the front, where one might expect the seriously interested customer, were still alarmingly empty. Felix may have been a little worried. But Felix was lucky. His lucky number was two, because the market value of an object is always determined by how badly more than one person wants it.

One of the people who wanted the book badly was Evangelos Venizelos, the Minister of Culture of Greece. He wanted it for his country. He had it publicly broadcast that it was Greece's moral, historic and scientific obligation to acquire the manuscript. At the last minute he organised a consortium to buy it, and the Greek Consul General in New York, Mr Manessis, was sent to the auction. He sat in the front row, together with an associate, on the left side of the room.

Just behind Mr Manessis was a man hoping to disappoint him – Simon Finch, a high-profile book dealer from London. If your idea of a bookseller is a bespectacled and tweedy English gentleman, then think again. Finch is nothing like that. About 45 years old, he looks more like a rock star than a bookman, and he sells books to rock stars quite as frequently as to libraries. Finch is the sort of man who can normally be found at book fairs wearing Vivienne Westwood suits and sporting designer stubble and dishevelled hair. He actually owns a pair of blue suede shoes. Finch is a romantic, and that's why he is in the book business. If you don't think that the combination of great history and supreme quality that books can provide is romantic, he will tell you that that's because you've never turned the pages of a great book. Five minutes later you might be a customer. When he went in to bid for the Palimpsest containing the treatises of Archimedes, Finch had more than his usual air of mystery. No one knew for whom he was acting, and no one knew quite how much that person was prepared to pay for the Archimedes Palimpsest.

At 2 p.m. the duel started, with Christie's Francis Wahlgren on the podium. The reserve price of $800,000 was quickly reached and the auction headed over the million-dollar milestone. Every time the Greeks raised their paddle – number 176 – high into the air, Finch would respond with his – number 169. The Greeks were on the telephone, taking instructions, and each time the price went up it would take them slightly longer to raise their paddle. Each time, Finch would top the new price. The Consul General answered to the call of $1,900,000 from the podium. Finch responded quickly to a call for $2,000,000. Wahlgren looked to the Consul General for a response to his request for any offers over $2,000,000. The Greeks were on the phone, desperately raising money. After what seemed like an eternity, Wahlgren brought down the hammer – 'Two million dollars it is,' he said. 'Paddle 169.' The Greeks had failed; the book had gone to Finch's unknown client. With the buyer's premium, the Archimedes Palimpsest had sold for $2,200,000.

This one book made just under half the amount of the combined total of all 501 lots of the Norman sale. No wonder its story hit the press. The next day, Finch's role was printed on the front page of the *New York Times* to an expectant world. He was the front man, not for a university, not for a library, but for an individual. But Finch would not tell all; he admitted only that the buyer was an American citizen who was 'not Bill Gates'. Felix de Marez Oyens had shown the book to Finch and the buyer before the sale. Felix had called it 'an old, dirty book', and brought it out of a brown-paper bag in his desk. This was not Felix's usual sales pitch, but it had worked. Whoever this individual was, unlike many eminent institutions, he wanted the book badly enough to take on a national government and a religious leader, and he was prepared to pay top dollar for the privilege of owning a mouldy, illegible, legally contentious old book. Was he a nutcase, intent on keeping secret knowledge to himself? Felix might have been happy, but many were outraged. If the Palimpsest's past was obscure, its future appeared dangerously uncertain.

BALTIMORE, MARYLAND

My name is Will Noel and I am a curator at the Walters Art Museum, in Baltimore, Maryland. The Walters, as it is always known, is a great American museum, modelled on a Renaissance palazzo in Genoa. Think grand marble staircases and a central courtyard surrounded by columns and you get the picture. It stands together with a number of other noble edifices around Mount Vernon Place in downtown Baltimore. In the centre of the square is a tall pillar surmounted by George Washington. If it were London, this square would be crowded with tourists, street musicians and students. But, located in inner-city Baltimore as it is, Mount Vernon Place is normally quite empty of people, lending it a sense of moody suspended animation that the passing traffic doesn't quite relieve. Inside this building is the superb collection of two individuals: father and son, William and Henry Walters. In a great act of civic philanthropy the collection was given by Henry to the City of Baltimore in 1934. Few people visit it, but the museum houses fifty-five centuries of art, and in many areas its holdings are truly fabulous. Thomas Hoving, the Director of the Metropolitan Museum of Art in New York, said of it: 'Piece for piece it is the greatest art museum in the United States.' It is my job to research into, teach from and exhibit the Walters collection of manuscripts and rare books. These are the stuff of legend and the fabric of history: they range in date from 300 BC to 1815, from an Egyptian Book of the Dead to Napoleon's memoirs. Most of them are medieval and sumptuously illuminated with images. Among the Walters' other holdings there are massive Roman sarcophagi, and paintings by Hugo van der Goes, Raphael, El Greco, Tiepolo and Manet.

Gary Vikan, the Director of the Walters, is my boss. Several weeks before the sale I had told Gary about the Archimedes Palimpsest – it is part of my job to follow the New York sales and Gary has a particular interest in medieval manuscripts. It struck a chord. When I walked into work the day after the sale, he hailed me down the grand stairway of the house that was once the Walters' home and, brandishing the *New York Times*, he said, 'Will! Why don't you find out who bought the Archimedes Palimpsest and see if you can get it for exhibition?'

I thought this was a bad idea. After all, the Walters is an art museum – it is concerned with what things look like. You cannot even see what is interesting about the Archimedes Palimpsest. I sent Gary a memo asking him if he really wanted me to do this. A couple of days later I got my memo back with a characteristic directorial scrawl: 'NOT WORTH MUCH WORK.' It was clear to me that I had at least to try. I had no more leads than anybody else. Simon Finch was the only name I had to run with, and so I asked Kathleen Stacey, the head librarian at the Walters, to find his email address on the web. This she did, and I sent Finch the following email:

> Dear Mr Finch,
>
> I am the manuscripts curator at the Walters Art Museum, Baltimore. The Walters has 850 medieval manuscripts, 1,300 incunables, and another 1,500 books printed after 1500. Most of these books are illustrated, and most of them were collected by Henry Walters between about 1895 and 1928 . . .
>
> We have an active acquisitions program, although our funding is limited. We have, for example, recently purchased a de luxe sixteenth-century Ethiopian manuscript from Sam Fogg. In general terms, therefore, I would be most interested in receiving

your catalogues, and would be grateful if you would add me to your mailing list.

However, I do have a more specific reason for writing. The Director of the Walters, Dr Gary Vikan, is a specialist in Greek material, and was fascinated (as am I) by the Archimedes Palimpsest. Dr Vikan wondered if there was any possibility of displaying the manuscript at the Walters for a short period of time. I do not know whether the purchaser of the volume would be at all interested in this idea. But if you think he might be, I would be most grateful to you if you could pass on the suggestion.

The Walters does have an active exhibition program. We are currently putting on a show of works from the Vatican; Monet came earlier in the year, and the Arts of Georgia are coming in 1999. If the owner of the Palimpsest were interested in putting the manuscript on view, he might consider that the Walters would be an appropriate place.

Please excuse this cold call. It is just a thought, but from our point of view an exciting one, given the extraordinary cultural importance of the codex. Whatever you think of this I would, as I say, look forward to hearing from you, and to receiving your catalogues. With many thanks for your time,

William Noel

Curator of Manuscripts and Rare Books

I moved my cursor to the top left of the screen: Send. The next minute I had dismissed it from my mind; frankly, the chances of anything resulting from this were remote in the extreme, I didn't even much want anything to happen, and I had labels to write for an exhibition of Dutch illuminated manuscripts. Still, I had done my job.

Emails are short on ritual. There is no walk to the letter box, no looking at the stamp, no slicing the envelope, no guessing the handwriting. They just pop up unbidden on your computer screen while you are engrossed in your daily business. Some of them, like little electronic terrorists, can blow your mind and change your life. Three days after my email to Finch this happened to me. I was happily writing an exhibition label for a book illuminated by the Masters of the Delft Grisailles when my computer went PING. You've got mail. Sam Fogg. Left Click:

Dear Will,

I am writing with reference to your letter to Simon Finch on the subject of the Palimpsest. I think the buyer of the Palimpsest is very sympathetic to the idea of sending the Archimedes to the Walters. I have already suggested to him that we visit the Museum in January. Perhaps we could discuss this and the Archimedes on the telephone soon.

Best wishes,
Sam Fogg

I sat motionless in my chair, eyes shut, with my hands over my head, rocking gently, my stomach turning to wax. Then I picked up the phone and dialled a number. It was a number I knew almost by heart. Although I hadn't been expecting to hear from him, I knew Sam Fogg well. As an unemployed postgraduate eking out an impoverished existence in Camden Town, London, I had once done some research on his behalf (for which read 'he employed me'), and when I became a curator in America I was in a position to acquire the odd manuscript from him. Sam is one of the art world's most colourful characters. Famous for having sold ceiling panels of Henry III of England's painted bedroom at Westminster to the British Museum, for having sold a leaf of Jan van Eyck's miniature masterpiece, the *Turin Milan Hours*, to the J. Paul Getty Museum, and for having bought a Rubens for £40,000,000, Sam is successful, smart and sexy. I don't remember the conversation well, but Sam must have told me that Simon Finch had rung him up because I had mentioned Sam to Finch in my email.

I arranged a flight to London. Before I caught the plane I discussed strategy with Gary. He thought that Simon Finch and Sam Fogg might actually be the same person, and that I was being given the runaround. I did not think so. Two days later I could prove it: I had lunch with both Simon Finch and Sam Fogg in Brown's restaurant on Maddox Street, London. It was only at this lunch that I discovered who the owner of the Palimpsest actually was. He had in fact been present at the auction, unnoticed by the competition and unrecognised by the press. He still likes to tell the story. Moreover, he had known exactly the liability that he was trying to buy and had bought it on the assumption that he would deposit it somewhere for conservation and scholarly study. His anonymity was important to him and hereafter he became known in any written correspondence as Mr B. We agreed that Sam and Mr B would visit the Walters in January.

This was just dandy. The trouble was I didn't really know anything about Archimedes, or his book. My brother Rob wrote a story about a dog-eared palimpsest once, and so I had the vague, romantic notion that palimpsests could harbour secret knowledge that you could get only if you were really smart. But that was all I could remember. I needed a few facts, and a map of the Mediterranean. I remember thinking that Archimedes was born on Samos, but I didn't know where Samos was. It took me a few days to find out that Archimedes was actually born in Sicily. What can I say? I had a lot to learn. I started reading. It was November. I had two months to learn enough not to look like a total idiot.

At about eleven o'clock on the morning of Tuesday, 19 January 1999 Mr B and Sam arrived at the museum. I met them at the entrance. Sam was a laugh a minute, as he always is; Mr B was completely silent. Nervously to start with, I took them up to the manuscript room, a climate-controlled vault that serves as my office as well as the repository of hundreds of medieval treasures. I entertained Sam and Mr B for an hour or so, before taking them to have lunch with Gary. I couldn't get a measure of the man. All I knew was that he was retiring, rich – richer than Croesus – and that he liked food. I knew he liked books too, but I wasn't learning anything more.

I had arranged lunch in a Baltimore institution – Marconi's, which is about four blocks from the Walters, on West Saratoga Street. A slightly down-at-heel survivor of Baltimore's elegant past, it serves wonderful food in a beautifully proportioned, white wooden-panelled room. On the way, Sam walked in front with Gary and I walked behind with Mr B, a nervous puppy trying to come to grips with the biggest fish of my little career. I remember congratulating him on his exciting new acquisition and saying that it was extremely generous of him to even consider putting his great new treasure on deposit at the Walters. His reaction to this was my first lesson in the mind of Mr B. He said that he had already left it on deposit with me. I did not understand. I asked him to say it again. He said that he had left it in a bag on my desk. I swallowed hard. As the museum registrar would have been quick to point out, this did not conform to standard museum protocols for the transportation and documentation of objects worth several millions of dollars. I went with the flow. Great, I told him, and what a good job it was that I had locked the door of my office on the way out.

Lunch was cordial, but a little odd to me. As I have said, Mr B enjoys his food, and he also likes taking his time. I wanted to go back to the museum and look at the manuscript. I was quite happy with one course; Mr B wanted his chocolate sundae. I could barely sit in my seat and I couldn't get Mr B out of his. Eventually lunch was over and the check was requested. Gary tried to pay with a credit card. This is Baltimore. Marconi's doesn't take American Express. I paid cash. Back we walked to the museum. I made my excuses on the way and ducked out to buy a pack of cigarettes. I hadn't had one for three hours and I smoked two in five minutes, pacing nervously. I caught up with them in time to turn the key to the manuscript room.

A lightweight blue bag was on my desk. Stamped in white on its side was a pair of scissors and, underneath them, the words GIANNI CAMPAGNA, MILANO. I unzipped the bag and pulled out a brown box. On the spine, in gold letters, was written: 'THE ARCHIMEDES PALIMPSEST'. I called my colleague Abigail Quandt, who is the Conservator of Manuscripts at the Walters. We opened the box. Inside was a small, thick book. The cover was of battered leather and badly stained. On the upper cover there was a flash of red paint and an odd silver-looking stud. Abigail placed the book between two velvet-covered blocks of wood on the table. The blocks prevented the manuscript from opening too far and placing unnecessary strain on the binding and the pages. She opened the book just far enough so that we could see inside. She kept the pages open by gently draping book 'snakes' over the edges of the pages. (These 'snakes' were actually curtain weights that are easily obtainable in John Lewis, a department store on Oxford Street in London; they work really well for keeping your place in a medieval book.) Mr B, Gary and I all peered over her shoulder. At first I saw nothing. Only slowly did my eyes adjust. And then the awesome thought dawned on me that I was looking at the unique key to the mind of a genius who had died 2,200 years earlier. I could barely see it to read it, and I would not have understood it if I could, but there it was nonetheless.

After a few minutes I grasped the fact that the time for gawking was over. Proper looking would have to come later. The museum registrar, Joan Elisabeth Reid, prepared a receipt for the book, which I handed over to Mr B. I took his email address, as email was, and remains, his preferred form of communication, and I said my goodbyes at the front entrance of the museum on North Charles Street. I then dashed back upstairs to the manuscript room, where Sam was still waiting, and I gave him an enormous and excited hug, forgetting for a moment that we were on live video feed and that Walters Security Staff were monitoring our every move.

Two days later I received a letter from the owner that contained a cheque made out to the Walters. It was big enough to get the institution's attention and me a pay raise.

★

Help for Archimedes

Mr B told me that he had bought an ugly book. Since he'd paid over two million for it, I took this with a pinch of salt. But no. Now that I had it in my hands I could see that he had played it straight this time. It was ugly. It was small – about the size of a standard bag of Domino sugar. When I opened it, I saw that the pages were mottled brown in colour. Matching tide-lines, caused by water, faced each other across page-openings. The pages tended to be brighter in the middle than around the edges, where they were more deeply stained. In fact right on their edges the pages were black, as if they had been in a fire. Overlaid upon the brown of the pages was stitched a grid pattern of slightly darker-brown Greek letters, which were all jumbled up. The monotony of the pages was only slightly relieved by the speckled red of the odd capital letter, and occasionally by purple stains of mould. When I turned pages, I could, just once in a while, make out the circles and straight lines of things that looked like diagrams that would, most inconveniently, disappear into the spine of the book from the inner margins. Compared to other manuscripts I had handled, the pages didn't flex very easily and they were contorted. Sometimes, as I was turning a page, it would suddenly 'pop' into a slightly different shape. Once in a while a whole page would just come out of the book in my hands. As I went through the book from start to finish, four pages stood out as having a certain charm because they had paintings on them, but overall it was a deflating experience. And then, towards the end, the pages looked so fragile and so mouldy that I shut it in alarm. This book, for which Mr B had paid so much, was on its last legs.

That is not a very helpful description, so let me describe the book etymologically. It is a manuscript book or, more technically, a manuscript codex. Derived from the Latin words *manu* (by hand) and *scriptus* (written), a manuscript is entirely written by hand. It is fundamentally different from a printed book in that it is not one of a large number of books printed as an edition. It is unique. Other manuscripts might contain some of the texts in it. All I knew for sure at this point was that no other manuscripts contained Archimedes' *Method*, *Stomachion*, or *Floating Bodies* in Greek. Secondly, this manuscript is a palimpsest. Derived from the Greek words *palin* (again) and *psan* (to rub), this means that the parchment used to make it has been scraped more than once. As we will see, to make parchment you need to scrape the skins of animals. If you want to reuse parchment that has already been used to make a book, you need to scrape the skin again to get rid of the old text before you write over it. This palimpsest manuscript consisted of 174 folios. Derived from the Latin *folium* (leaf), a folio has a front and back – a recto and a verso – that are equivalent to modern pages. The folios were numbered 1 through 177 but, mysteriously, three numbers were missing. I hoped Mr B knew that he was missing some folios.

The manuscript is now called the Archimedes Palimpsest, but this is a bit confusing. Make no mistake: the manuscript *is* a prayer book. It looks like a prayer book, it feels like a prayer book, it even smells like a prayer book, and it is prayers that you see on its folios. It is only called the Archimedes Palimpsest because folios taken from an earlier manuscript containing treatises by Archimedes were used to make it. But remember, the Archimedes text has been scraped off. Note, too, that the scribes of the prayer book used the folios taken from several other earlier manuscripts as well as the Archimedes manuscript. At the time of the sale nobody had a clue what was on these folios; they didn't look like folios from the Archimedes manuscript and they didn't look as if they were all from the same manuscript. For example, while the Archimedes text was laid out in two columns, the texts on other palimpsest folios were laid out in one column, others had a different number of lines per folio and the handwriting on these folios, when it wasn't invisible, was sometimes very different. Mr B had bought several different books in one. Basically, I concluded, the Archimedes Palimpsest was only called the Archimedes Palimpsest because no one could identify the other texts in the manuscript and because the Archimedes texts were considered so much more important than the prayer book that was on top of them.

But how important, really, was this 'Archimedes Palimpsest'? I began to ask around, and Mr B's book got decidedly mixed reviews. Even though it made $2.2 million at auction, the truth was that only three parties had put up a fight for it: the patriarchate, the Greek government and Mr B. None of them knew all that much about Archimedes. How come, I asked, no academic institution was sufficiently interested in it to enter the fray? I found out that many well-informed scholars were sceptical that we could learn much more from this book. Everybody kept mentioning that someone called Heiberg had discovered the manuscript and read it in 1906. And Heiberg, apparently, was something of a god. It was unlikely that he would have missed anything important, they said. Mr B, they told me, had bought a relic, but not a book that would reward much further research.

Still, Mr B had entrusted his relic to me and I had no choice but to take his new possession as seriously as he did. His book clearly needed three things: first, since it was literally falling apart, it needed conservation; second, since no one could see the text in it properly, it needed advanced imaging; third, if by any chance Heiberg had missed a few lines, then scholars needed to read it. I knew that Mr B would require the best. This was good, because his book was such a wreck that it needed the best – the best conservators, the most advanced imaging and the most highly qualified scholars. I was none of these things, and I wondered whether I was the right person to be looking after Mr B's book. I am extremely clumsy; I once possessed a Kodak instamatic but have long since lost it; my expertise is in Latin manuscripts, not Greek ones, religious books, not mathematical ones, and beautiful books, not ugly ones. Certainly legible books, for goodness sake, and not invisible ones.

That Mr B should have chosen me, of all people, to look after his book seemed more than a little absurd to me. But Mr B knew my limitations. My job, as he saw much more clearly than I at the time, was not to do the work, but to get the right people to do it. But how was I to go about doing even that?

THE PROJECT MANAGER

On Friday, 16 July 1999 the *Washington Post* published an article on the Palimpsest. Abigail and I received many emails in reaction to it. Some are among the most zany I have ever received. (To the unacknowledged grandson of Rasputin I can only say that I have not yet found any corroboration of your pedigree in the Archimedes Palimpsest.) Let's concentrate on the ones we found helpful. Here's the best of them.

> Dear Drs Noel and Quandt
>
> I read with interest the article in the *Washington Post*. Congratulations. It certainly puts our work in perspective. We in the intelligence community have equipment that may be able to help. We also have a wide range of contacts in the imaging community that could prove useful to you. If you would like to discuss this further, please do not hesitate to get in touch. Whatever the case, it sounds like a fascinating project. Good luck in your endeavors.
>
> Yours sincerely,
> Michael B. Toth
> National Policy Director
> National Reconnaissance Office

The National Reconnaissance Office (NRO) is not a secret any more, but it was for a long time. Mr B told me that the only reason it was forced to become public is that people could not understand why hundreds of cars were disappearing into a small office building. The answer was that most of it was underground and that it was the unacknowledged nerve centre of the US reconnaissance satellite programme. Now, though, you can find details on the web: working with the CIA and the Department of Defense, it can warn of potential trouble spots around the world, help plan military operations and monitor the environment. Its mission is to develop and operate unique and innovative space-reconnaissance systems and conduct intelligence-related activities essential for US national security. As an avid John le Carré reader, I had always been enthralled with the world of espionage. This was too cool.

I phoned Mr Toth. I was tempted to say that, if he hung on just a moment, I would take the book up on to the roof of the museum, and if he could just fly a satellite over we could all be finished in a few minutes. More soberly, I invited him up from Washington to Baltimore. I was still hoping that he would have a piece of kit, maybe in his back pocket, maybe disguised as a watch, that could help me with my problem. Much to my disappointment, it soon became clear that no government agency could help us in the imaging of the Palimpsest. Since it was private property, the tax dollars of the American public could not be spent on it. Mike said that he would nonetheless be happy to help us as a volunteer. Deprived of his toys, I was not sure how he could, but it seemed unwise to annoy this man, and he seemed pretty certain that he would be useful.

Mike, it turned out, was an expert at managing highly technical systems, including imaging systems, and particularly in assessing something called 'program risk'. This was an amazing stroke of fortune. I had, apparently, found an American who was professionally trained to tell me exactly how much trouble I was in. He'd seen worse, but I'd better shape up. More importantly, he was willing to help me. I am a scholar who specialises in illuminated liturgical manuscripts from Canterbury, England, of about 1020. I have a few skills. I can, for example, recite the Book of Psalms backwards and the kings and queens of England forwards, from Hengist through to Henry VIII. But these skills are not particularly well suited to running an effective integrated project at a reasonable cost, to the correct level of performance, and on a practical schedule, in order to produce value for an owner and an Archimedes text for the world. Boy, did I need a technical consultant, preferably one who, I liked to believe, had pressed the 'go' button to launch a space shuttle.

Mike, like so many people who were to help with Archimedes, was a volunteer. He didn't want money and he didn't want his government service celebrated by the press. In fact, his work on Archimedes was all done through his father's company, R. B. Toth Associates, and that was how he was introduced to people. With Mike on board, everybody else got a cover as well, or so it seemed to me. Mr B became the 'source selection authority' (that is, he decided everything); Abigail became the 'critical path' (that is, everything depended on conservation); the scholars became the 'end-users' (that is, they defined what was best); and the imagers became the 'value added' (that is, they made the difference). And me? Mike gave me the very grand title of 'Project Director'.

THE SOURCE SELECTION AUTHORITY

I know the owner of the Archimedes Palimpsest. I know him very well. If you don't know him by now, then you don't need to. To the press I say he's more use to you as an enigma; to the curious I say mind your own bloody business. To those who do know him, he is a loyal, generous, thoughtful and enlightened man. His email style is a bit short, but you get used to it.

When the Archimedes Palimpsest was sold, some scholars were outraged that the book went back into a private collection. But if Archimedes had meant enough to the public, then public institutions would have bought him. Archimedes did not; public institutions were offered it at a lower price than it actually fetched at auction and they turned it down. If you think this is a shame, then it is a shame that you share. We all live in a world where value translates into cash. If you care about what happens to world heritage, then get political about it, and be prepared to pay for it. Sorry.

The practical reasons why it might have been a 'bad thing' that the manuscript went into a private collection are that the book might have been badly handled and the right scholars might not have got to look at it. Someone could just have tossed it into their attic. As we will see, given the state in which it came out of the last private collection, these were valid concerns. I hope, by the end of this book, if not by the end of this chapter, to have demonstrated that this manuscript has been cared for extremely well and that the right people have looked at it. Another reason why it might have been a 'bad thing' is that its future was uncertain. This remains true: when the work is done, the manuscript will go back to the owner, and I do not know what will happen to it. But the best predictor of future behaviour is past behaviour, and over the last seven years the owner has behaved responsibly, thoughtfully and generously.

What do I mean by this? Well, he is extremely interested in the Archimedes Palimpsest and greatly concerned with the project and its goals. He is knowledgeable about books, he cares about them, and he has a superb library. He does make all the important decisions with regard to the book, but he does so after having very carefully listened to us and read proposals that I have forwarded to him. And what's more, he pays for all the work to be done. The project has never suffered for lack of money. Manuscript scholars, classicists and mathematicians owe a great deal to the owner of the Archimedes Palimpsest.

THE CRITICAL PATH

The first thing was to secure the well-being of the manuscript. Whatever else happened, the manuscript had to stay safe. Here I did not have to do anything, and have done nothing ever since the book arrived. Abigail Quandt has had to do it all. Abigail has an international reputation for the conservation of medieval manuscripts. She has worked on some of the world's most famous manuscripts, including the Dead Sea Scrolls and one of the greatest masterpieces of the Middle Ages – the Book of Hours of Jeanne D'Evreux at the Metropolitan Museum of Art. Abigail had her training in Dublin with Tony Cains, Head of Conservation at Trinity College Dublin, and in England with Roger Powell, who rebound the Book of Kells. She had been at the Walters much longer than I – since 1984. I was the new kid on the block.

Abigail was integral to the planning of Archimedes' future, and in any of the decisions concerning the well-being of the manuscript – and there were to be many – Abigail's voice was always the strongest. I didn't just have a great colleague in my work. More importantly, I was totally convinced that Archimedes was in the safest possible hands. I could rest assured that I wouldn't make the situation worse for Archimedes, and I could concentrate on other things.

THE END-USERS

I received many offers to help with the decipherment of the Palimpsest by a variety of enthusiasts. Some of these offers were rather forceful (this is an understatement). I tried not to be offensive while I worked out a strategy. The manuscript was so fragile that I could not let just anyone have a crack at it. I needed to get the two or three people who could best edit the texts, so that they could be published. The question was which two or three?

Gary Vikan immediately advised me to get in touch with Nigel Wilson, of Lincoln College, Oxford. He was an obvious choice for two reasons. The first was that he knew the book better than anyone else, having contributed a great deal to the catalogue of the manuscript that was produced for the Christie's auction. Christie's asked him to catalogue it for the same reason as I wanted him to work on it: he was without peer in scholarship on the transmission of classical texts from antiquity through the Middle Ages, and his palaeographical (script-deciphering) and philological (text-analysing) skills are legendary. I wrote to him on the Monday, 25 January 1999 explaining that if we were to do justice to the manuscript we needed a distinguished scholar who knew about the subject to be our adviser and that, if he was willing, he was in this respect uniquely placed to help us. Ever since then Nigel has been helping us. He has become far more than an independent adviser.

Next I phoned my very discreet friend Patrick Zutshi, Keeper of

Manuscripts and University Archives at Cambridge University Library, and spoke to him of my problem. He advised me to get in touch with Patricia Easterling, who was Regius Professor of Greek at Cambridge University. This was pretty grand for me, but not, I thought, for Archimedes. So I rang her up and said, 'Can you please tell me who is the best person to study the Archimedes Palimpsest?' I met her in early March 1999 in the tea room of the University Library, and she suggested I get in touch with Reviel Netz, who was translating Archimedes into English for Cambridge University Press. Netz, she said, would be more interested in it than most. While many were sceptical about the discoveries that could be made from the text, all agreed that the manuscript was important for its diagrams, and Netz seemed to have a particular thing for diagrams (more of which later). Netz was at the Massachusetts Institute of Technology. I wrote him an email, and then I got him on the phone. Pat Easterling was right:

'Yes. I need to see the diagrams, particularly for *Sphere and Cylinder*,' I think were the first words out of his mouth. I am still not sure because he has a rather thick Israeli accent. That's a bit pushy, I thought, and I tried to put the brakes on. So I spoke slowly, and painted a broad picture of what our work might be and how he might fit into it, and, if he was interested, then perhaps, just perhaps, he should come to Baltimore in the fullness of time.

When I met him off the gate at the airport a couple of days later, I understood immediately that his pushiness was induced by his fear and his excitement. I did my best to calm his fear: yes, the Walters was a centre of excellence; no, the Palimpsest wasn't here for a passing visit; yes, he could look at it – tomorrow, even – but he had to be very careful; no, I didn't plan to show it to just anyone. By the next day I understood where he was coming from: he knew better than anyone else that the box containing the Palimpsest contained a time machine to Archimedes in Syracuse in the third century BC. He explained the importance of the diagrams to me, as no one else ever has. Having convinced himself that I understood the grave responsibility that was on my shoulders, he looked at me with sympathy. He knew that I was going to do my best for the book, even though I did not understand it and even though it would be a long and demanding task that would take me away from my own research for years. Good. He was on my side, if only because I was on Archimedes' side.

Unlike me, Reviel has never thought of the Palimpsest as ugly – he doesn't care about its looks; he simply regards the Palimpsest with awe, and he felt daunted by the task ahead of him. His doubts were gone, though, when he heard that he would be working side by side with a colleague of the stature of Nigel Wilson. Reviel had another suggestion too. He thought it important to get someone to work just on those folios of the Palimpsest that contained texts not by Archimedes. He wanted to know who kept Archimedes company in this prayer book. I thought this was a good idea: even if the text of Archimedes was well understood, there was the chance that we could find out more about the other palimpsested texts.

The name Reviel suggested was Natalie Tchernetska, a Latvian who was doing her PhD at Trinity College, Cambridge, on Greek palimpsests. Pat Easterling was her supervisor. Small world. I met her in Pat's rooms in Newnham College in the summer of 1999. She was helpful in assessing the images and we will have a reason to look at some of her work later. This was the core of the academic team that was to go on to paint an entirely new picture of the greatest mathematician of antiquity and to reveal the world's greatest palimpsest.

THE VALUE ADDED

One day in August 1999 I sat down beside Abigail in my office and faced Mike Toth. We had to find the right people to image the Palimpsest. This was intimidating. I felt overwhelmed with the thought of how much work I would have to do, but so totally ignorant that I didn't even know precisely what this work would be. Mike thought that we should arrange a competition for people to image the Palimpsest. I thought this was a bad idea: it seemed like a lot of work. Mike gently insisted: it would greatly increase the number of imaging procedures that we could perform on the book and it would give the participants the incentive to reduce costs and increase performance in the hope that they would be rewarded with the commission for imaging the entire volume. This was merely sensible, he said. It sounded like rocket science to me. Then he told me for the first time about a Request for Proposals. An RFP is quite standard to me now. It is a document in which you outline the problem and ask for a solution.

Abigail drew up the RFP. It is one of a number of thorough and brilliant documents that she has written through the history of the project. It started with a goal: to digitally retrieve and preserve for posterity all the writings in the 174 folios of the Archimedes Palimpsest. It mentioned all the constraints: because the manuscript was very fragile, all the handling of the manuscript would be undertaken by Abigail and personnel that she designated. It outlined the phases of work: after the competitive phase, the selected contractor would image the entire manuscript in a disbound state. The whole proposal ran to six pages. In response to the RFP we received six proposals. Of these six we submitted three before Mr B, and of these three Mr B selected two for the competition.

One team consisted of Roger Easton, a faculty member at the Chester F. Carlson Center for Imaging Science at the Rochester Institute of Technology, and Keith Knox, who at the time was the Principal Scientist at the Xerox Digital Imaging Technology Centre, also in Rochester, although he now works for Boeing, in Hawaii. Keith, together with Brian J. Thompson, had achieved fame years earlier by developing and patenting a method – the Knox–Thompson Algorithm – that recovers images from telescopic photographs that have been degraded by the atmosphere. More recently, Roger and Keith had formed a team, together with the late Robert H. Johnston, to image degraded texts, including a palimpsest in Princeton University Library and several of the Dead Sea Scroll fragments. Their work had already been celebrated on the BBC and on American TV.

They had already done some work on the Palimpsest, as Keith's sister-in-law knew Hope Mayo, who had worked with Nigel to prepare the catalogue for the Christie's sale. Some of their images are actually in the catalogue. Roger, Keith and Bob Johnston were a known quantity and a safe bet.

The other team was from Johns Hopkins University and was, in effect, one man, William A. Christens-Barry. Bill is not an imaging scientist, still less a photographer; he is a physicist. At the time we met him he was working at the Applied Physics Laboratory of Johns Hopkins University. APL employs nearly three thousand engineers, information technologists and scientists. It works primarily on development projects funded by federal agencies. Foremost among these are the US Navy and NASA. Scientists at APL participate in the entire range of data collection and analysis activities of interest to its sponsors, including data from air-, ocean-, and space-borne reconnaissance and imaging platforms. Work in non-defence, non-space areas constitutes a secondary activity of the laboratory. Most of Bill's research pertained to problems in biological and medical science, particularly in relation to cancer. Impressive place; impressive guy. His proposal was full of ideas that no one else had thought of.

THE PROJECT DIRECTOR

All these people had well-defined roles. What was I? I was Archimedes' factotum. I did the talking and I did the arranging. As Mike put it, I kept an awful lot of plates spinning on their poles. And I was going to have to do it for a long time. Unlike all the others, I had no special qualifications for my role. I was just a chipper guy who liked books. Nonetheless, and even if it was more by luck than by judgement, I had talked to the right people and I had arranged a lot. By the end of the year I had a plan in place and the key players were on board. I could say what I was doing to anybody who called. I just couldn't really say why I was doing it. If you had called me up and asked me why any of the Friends of Archimedes wanted to do this work, I would immediately have referred you to Reviel Netz.

2

Archimedes in Syracuse

Archimedes is the most important scientist who ever lived.

This conclusion can be reached as follows. The British philosopher A. N. Whitehead once said, famously: 'The safest general characterisation of the European philosophical tradition is that it consists of a series of footnotes to Plato.' This judgement may sound outrageous, but in fact it is quite sober-minded. Plato's immediate followers, such as Aristotle, tried above all to refute, or to refine, Plato's arguments. Later philosophers debated whether one should best follow Plato or Aristotle. And so, in a real sense, all later Western philosophy is but footnotes to Plato.

The safest general characterisation of the European scientific tradition is that it consists of a series of footnotes to Archimedes – by which I mean roughly the same kind of genealogy that Whitehead meant for Plato. As an example we need only look at one of the most influential books of modern science, Galileo's *Discourses Concerning Two New Sciences*. This book was published in 1638, by which time Archimedes had been dead for exactly 1,850 years, a very long time indeed. Yet Galileo, throughout, is in debt to Archimedes. Essentially, Galileo advances the two sciences of statics (how objects behave in rest) and dynamics (how objects behave in motion). For statics, Galileo's principal tools are *centres of gravity* and the *law of the balance*. Both of these concepts Galileo borrows – explicitly, always expressing his admiration – from Archimedes. For dynamics, Galileo's principal tools are the *approximation of curves*, and the *proportions of times and motions*, both of which, once again, derive directly from Archimedes.

No other authority is as frequently quoted, or quoted with equal reverence. Galileo essentially started out from where Archimedes had left off, proceeding in the same direction as that defined by his Greek predecessor. This is true not only of Galileo but also of the other great figures of the so-called 'scientific revolution', such as Leibniz, Huygens, Fermat, Descartes and Newton. All of them were Archimedes' children. With Newton, the science of the scientific revolution reached its perfection, in a perfectly Archimedean form. Based on pure, elegant first principles, applying pure geometry, Newton deduced the rules governing the universe. All of later science is a consequence of the desire to generalise Newtonian – that is, Archimedean – methods.

The two principles that the authors of modern science learned from Archimedes were:

- The mathematics of infinity
- The application of mathematical models to the physical world

Thanks to the Palimpsest, we now know much more about these two aspects of Archimedes' achievement.

The mathematics of infinity and the application of mathematical models to the physical world are closely interrelated. This is because physical reality consists of infinitesimal pulses of force acting instantaneously. As a consequence, to find out about the outcome of such forces, we need to sum up infinitely many 'pulses', each infinitesimally small. This is surprising: we might think that the mathematics of infinity is some kind of flight-of-fancy of no practical application (after all, we might think there is no infinity to be met with in the ordinary world). But it turns out that the mathematics of infinity is the most practical tool of science, so important that it is often called simply 'the calculus'. The application of mathematics to the physical world, via the calculus: this, in a formula, is modern science. Newton, in particular, used the calculus, in implicit form, to work out how the planets behave – a beautiful result, the inspiration for all later science and, at bottom, the application of Archimedean insights.

And so, since Archimedes led, more than anyone else, to the formation of the calculus, and since he was the pioneer of the application of mathematics to the physical world, it turns out that, indeed, Western science is but a series of footnotes to Archimedes. Thus it turns out also that Archimedes was the most important scientist who ever lived.

Archimedes' influence was not confined to the contents of his science: there is a special quality about his writings. Again and again, his readers are shocked by the delightful surprise of an unexpected combination. Elegant, unanticipated juxtapositions were Archimedes' staple, and the main reason later scientists were so influenced by him was that he was such a pleasure to read. Later mathematicians, directly or indirectly, all tried to imitate Archimedes' surprise and elegance, so that our very sense of what a mathematical treatise should aim at is shaped by Archimedes' example. In the following chapters, I shall try to explain not only the contents of Archimedes' works – his contributions to the calculus and to mathematical physics – but also his style. Both are equally worthy of our admiration.

I gradually came to appreciate both these aspects of Archimedes' achievement – the contents and the style – while working on the Archimedes Palimpsest. A major discovery made in 2001 made us see, for the first time, how close Archimedes was to modern concepts of infinity. Another major discovery, made in 2003, made me rethink our entire conception of Archimedes' style. Such was the work on the Palimpsest, throughout: laboriously poring over a manuscript page (or, more often, over its enhanced image on the laptop screen); the letters forming into words, into phrases; usually nothing new; occasionally discoveries, sometimes of important historical significance; and then – twice – discoveries that shook the foundations of the history of mathematics.

I never thought that I should ever find myself laboriously poring over manuscript pages. The work of editing the major texts from antiquity, based on the transcription of medieval manuscripts, was mostly done in the nineteenth century. Of course, one could always make small improvements or one could edit minor authors, but not many people do this kind of work today. This is not only because the more interesting authors are already edited. The intellectual climate today is very different from what it was in the nineteenth century. Nowadays people are less interested in the dry details of texts and more in the syntheses based on those texts. A PhD thesis in Classics is usually, today, some kind of theoretical reflection upon the established texts, rather than an addition to the texts themselves. 'Theory' is what people look for: put bluntly, you're not likely to get a job if your intellectual output is made only of textual editions. Nor is this necessarily a bad development. Nineteenth-century scholarship was very impressive and we owe it a great deal, but it does sometimes make for very boring reading (often in Latin, at that), and it is even naïve, occasionally, in its lack of critical and theoretical reflection. Our understanding of the ancient world was made much richer and more profound by the application of insights from cultural anthropology, for instance, or from general poetics and linguistics. My own PhD thesis, prepared at Cambridge under the supervision of Sir Geoffrey Lloyd – the doyen of Greek science – was very much part of this modern tradition. I was greatly inspired by Geoffrey Lloyd's application of anthropology to the study of Greek thought, as well as by his comparative method (where he puts Greek science side by side with its Chinese counterpart). My first book, *The Shaping of Deduction in Greek Mathematics: a Study in Cognitive History*, involved specifically the application of insights from cognitive science (or the other way around: my own hope is that cognitive scientists would find something to learn from what historians have to tell them). My object throughout was to uncover the mathematical experience: how does it register in the mind's eye? To get a sense of this, I was persuaded, one must be able to read the mathematics in accurate translation, which carefully follows the author's formulations, because they convey to us how the ancients themselves thought about their science. Now the most important of them all was never translated into English. For Archimedes there existed only T. L. Heath's poor paraphrase written in

1897, which simply ignores Archimedes' mathematical language. I therefore decided to produce a new translation, with a commentary that incorporates my own theoretical angle on Greek mathematics.

I was going to do more than just translate Archimedes. I am one of a number of scholars who, very recently, have begun to pay attention to the visual aspect of science. I mentioned that nineteenth-century scholarship may appear, in some respects, outdated, and here is one respect having to do with the editing work itself. The scholars who edited mathematical texts in the nineteenth century were so interested in the *words* that they ignored the *images*. If you open an edition from that era, the diagrams you find are not based upon what is actually drawn in the original manuscripts. The diagrams represent, instead, the editor's own drawing. I was shocked to realise that and began to consider: should I produce, for the first time, an edition of the diagrams? I knew that this would involve travel to the major libraries housing Archimedes' various manuscripts. I looked for where those manuscripts were. It turned out that they were in Paris, Florence, Venice and Rome. Well, why not? I decided that this was a good idea.

This was a very ambitious project, and not an altogether likely one. There are some 100,000 words of Archimedes to be translated. Difficult 100,000 words. Worse: as friends kept pointing out to me, what was I to do where the text was uncertain? How was I to decide, given that the most important manuscript was *no longer available*?

Because, you see, there it was – the Archimedes Palimpsest, the unique source for *Floating Bodies*, *Method* and *Stomachion* and a crucial piece of evidence for most other works – and no one knew where it was. It had been studied at the beginning of the twentieth century – and then disappeared. Nor did I expect it to resurface – which was my reply to my friends: since the manuscript is likely to remain unavailable, let us just proceed as if it did not exist, otherwise we will never do anything regarding Archimedes.

Pat Easterling, the Regius Professor of Greek at Cambridge and an expert on Greek manuscripts, closely followed my project, teaching me the basic skills of palaeography. One day I received a letter from her. The letter said that Christie's were asking permission to photograph a certain leaf kept at Cambridge University Library, because this leaf was believed to have been taken out from the Archimedes Palimpsest, a manuscript that they were about to sell.

I then mentioned this casually to my colleagues in ancient science, assuming they had known about this all along. No one did. This letter from Pat Easterling was a bombshell: the news of the imminent sale suddenly broke into the community of Archimedes scholars. The rest is history. Will has already mentioned his own meeting with Pat Easterling and his email to me. And as for my reaction upon the receipt of this email – that is, as for my wild, childish, embarrassing cries of jubilation . . . of this I prefer not to speak. Let us speak of Archimedes.

Who was Archimedes?

The Second Punic War (218–202 BC) was, to antiquity, much like the Second World War was to the modern era. This was a cataclysmic catastrophe of unprecedented proportions, turning the geopolitics of the Mediterranean upside down. For a moment, it appeared as if Hannibal might conquer Rome – yet it survived, triumphant, so powerful at the end of the war that the entire Mediterranean was at its mercy. The independence of Greek states was gone, the civilisation that Archimedes represented had been humbled. One of the major turning points of the war came as Syracuse fell. This, the leading Greek city in the western Mediterranean, had made the wrong strategic decision of allying itself with the Carthaginians. In 212, following a long siege, its defences – set up by Archimedes and undefeated in battle – succumbed to treachery. We do not know how: Archimedes died.

The above, in point of fact, sums up what we know of Archimedes as a historical person. It should be stressed that we are lucky to know even that; indeed we should be amazed that we can date events in antiquity at all. After all, no one in antiquity jotted down: 'Archimedes died in 212 BC'! The way ancient dates are obtained is fundamentally as follows: we are lucky to possess several historical documents from antiquity arranged as annals, i.e. detailing events year by year (the Roman author Livy is a famous example). Their dating system was different from ours, but occasionally such authors provide us with astronomical data (eclipses, in particular). We can then apply Newtonian physics to calculate the date of those events, and by such calculations we gain footholds on ancient chronology, constructing the basic equivalences between ancient dates and modern ones. Without such astronomical data no chronology could be fixed with any certainty. Even for the date of his death it is the science due to Archimedes that allows us to learn about Archimedes himself.

The siege of Syracuse was a major event, etched into ancient memory. It was in all the annals and we know very well when it ended. The figure of Archimedes himself, as the chief Syracusan engineer, was of great fascination to his contemporaries, and it appears again and again in ancient accounts. (This, once again, is a little like the Second World War: think of the way Einstein got etched into the public imagination as 'the father of the atom bomb'.) This then is safe: we do know when Archimedes died. But other pieces of evidence are much less reliable. Archimedes' dates are often reported in encyclopedias as 287–212 BC. We know where the 212 comes from. What about the 287? This is based on a later Greek author, who mentions that Archimedes died 'as an old man, 75 years old' – fine as it goes, only that the author in question, Johannes Tzetzes, lived in the twelfth century AD(!). What he has to say on Archimedes comes from a gossipy, fanciful poem. This, for instance, is our main source for the story according to which Archimedes invented mirrors that burned enemy ships. Surely, Archimedes' contemporaries would have reported such a thing had it happened and Tzetzes was a Byzantine, whose navy was indeed famous for its ship-burning feats. In short, Tzetzes' story is just that – a story – and he makes his Archimedes an old man just for literary effect. Probably Archimedes was quite old (so says the reliable Polybius), but nothing more is known.

Here is the problem: Archimedes was so famous, legends would cling to him. And now, how are we to separate history from legend? This is the historian's problem. Up until the nineteenth century it was common to accept ancient stories as reality; since then, scepticism has reigned. Perhaps historians today are too cautious, but we tend to dismiss nearly everything that is said about Archimedes. Did he cry '*Eureka*'? I doubt this myself, and let me explain why. Let's take the most famous version of this story (also the earliest) told by Vitruvius – a date and author which already give room for doubt. Vitruvius writes some two hundred years after Archimedes' death and is not a very reliable historian in general (his book is a manual of architecture, which he spices up with historical anecdotes).

Here is the story. Archimedes is lost in thought contemplating the problem of a crown. This crown is supposed to be made of gold – but is it pure? Then Archimedes notices the water splashing out of the bath . . . and immediately he runs out crying '*Eureka, eureka*' – *Eureka* just what, precisely? According to Vitruvius, *eureka* is the observation that the volume of water displaced by a body immersed in it is equal to the volume of the body itself: so put the crown in water, measure what may be called the 'splashed' quantity – and you have the volume of the crown. Compare this to an equally heavy mass of gold: does it make the same splash? The heavier it is, the less splash it makes. So now you know whether the crown has the specific gravity of gold or not. The method is sound, but it is based on a trivial observation – essentially, that 'bigger things make bigger splashes'. This is so trivial as not to be mentioned at all in Archimedes' own treatise on *Floating Bodies* (whose unique Greek version survives in the Palimpsest).

To me it appears that Vitruvius, or his previous source, knew that Archimedes discovered something about bodies immersed in water, and was also familiar with some trivial, pre-scientific observations (such as that 'bigger things make bigger splashes'), and then invented a story to tie the two. But he clearly knew nothing about Archimedes' science. This is the pattern with all of the stories told of Archimedes, from Vitruvius to Tzetzes: they appear to be urban legends. Sorry.

Some pieces of real evidence can be put together, providing us with the outlines of a fascinating story. As we shall see again and again through this book, the pieces of evidence can be extremely minuscule, and then call for lots of interpretation. And this holds for the most important piece of biographical evidence we have for Archimedes. This piece of evidence is an aside, made in the course of one of Archimedes' more surprising works, the *Sand-Reckoner*. In this treatise Archimedes notes various estimates that were offered for the ratio of the sun to the moon: Eudoxus, for instance, said the sun was nine times bigger and then – so our manuscripts read – some 'Pheidias Acoupater' said the sun was *twelve* times bigger. Now there is no such name or place as 'Acoupater'. The text reads literally *pheidia tou akoupatros*, but bear in mind that, until quite late in the Middle Ages, Greek was written without spaces between the words. This gives rise to the following conjecture: if we separate the words differently (which we are always allowed to do in interpreting ancient Greek texts), and change just one letter, the gibberish 'acoupater' can make perfect sense. The reason we are allowed to make such corrections is that certainly mistakes were made by scribes as they copied their texts – our manuscripts are full of such scribal errors. And so the suggestion was made, by several editors in the nineteenth century, to reread with the '*k*' changed to '*m*', and a space inserted: *pheidia tou amou patros*. This is 'Pheidias, my father'. You can see that this is a thin thread, but a very robust one: the text *has* to be corrected, and the correction offered is so elegant and straightforward it seems as if it *has* to be true.

On this thin thread hangs the entire family biography of Archimedes, which should give a sense of how important – and how difficult – the detailed study of manuscripts is. All of our knowledge of the ancient world is derived from the patient, laborious piecing together of jigsaw puzzles such as that. The above does not seem like much – but it does tell us that Archimedes' father was an astronomer, and that his name was Phidias.

This is a fact I find very meaningful. I have studied the name 'Pheidias' in antiquity, and I ask you to bear in mind two facts: (a) art, as well as craftsmanship in general, were not very highly appreciated by the ancient aristocrats (who generally speaking looked down on anyone dirtying his hands); (b) Pheidias is the name of the most famous artist in antiquity – the master sculptor of the Parthenon of the fifth century BC. Now, with these two facts in mind, I ask you to consider the following observation: *elsewhere, when we can tell what a person called 'Pheidias' did, it typically turns out he was an artist of some sort.* This is quite simple: the name Pheidias would be bestowed on your son – as a proud prophecy – only in artists' families. Otherwise, why give a name that has the lowly associations of craftsmanship? So let us note this fact, as well: Archimedes' grandfather was an artist.

We have not yet exhausted the quarry of names. What about the name Archimedes itself? This is, in fact, unique – and uniquely appropriate to Archimedes. It is made of two components (as is very often the case with Greek names): *arche*, or 'principle, rule, number one', and *medos*, or 'mind, wisdom, wit'. The name means, if read from the beginning to end, 'the number one mind', which is a very good description of Archimedes. But it was probably meant to be read from the end to the beginning (as is more often done with Greek names). It is a unique name, but it has a parallel in another name, Diomedes, with 'Dio' (a variant of 'Zeus') instead of *arche*. The name Diomedes means 'The Mind of Zeus', and the name Archimedes therefore means 'The Mind of the Principle' – which sounds a bit strange but makes perfect sense. Greek philosophers in the generations before Archimedes, starting with such figures as Plato, gradually evolved a kind of monotheistic, scientific religion in which they worshipped not so much the anthropomorphic gods of Greek religion but rather the beauty and order of the cosmos, its 'principle'. The name Archimedes suggests, therefore, that Pheidias – the astronomer, Archimedes' father – subscribed to such a religion and worshipped the beauty and the order in the cosmos. So we can tell quite a lot about Archimedes' background – all based on tiny pieces of evidence and lots of interpretation. The grandfather, an artist; the father, a scientist – an astronomer who turns to the new religion of beauty and order in the cosmos; and then the son in whose works art and science, beauty and order all work together in perfect harmony.

Those works are of course the key to understanding Archimedes. The stories may be urban legends, but the works are there for us to read, and the surprising thing is that, dry mathematical pieces as they might seem to be, they actually burst with personality. In his pure science, Archimedes keeps splashing out of the bath. Art and science, beauty and order: let us begin to see how they come together in Archimedes' works.

Science before Science

When we say that 'Archimedes was a scientist', we may be tempted to imagine him wearing a white coat, contemplating vials with purplish liquids – well, this is not what he did. He was wearing a tunic, contemplating diagrams drawn on sand. And then, we may be tempted to imagine him as a very earnest man, dedicated entirely to the cause of impersonal truth. This, too, would be as wrong as the purplish vials. Archimedes was not a modern scientist. His was a different kind of science: a science from before our own, professionalised, capital-letter 'Science'.

Perhaps the best introduction to the man is in what he tells us in the introduction to one of his treatises, *On Spiral Lines*. The introduction is presented as a letter to a colleague, Dositheus, and Archimedes begins by reminding Dositheus of previous letters. You will recall, says Archimedes, that I have put forth a number of mathematical puzzles. I announced various discoveries and asked for other mathematicians to find their own proofs of those discoveries. Well (notes Archimedes, somewhat triumphantly) – no one did! Then again, continues

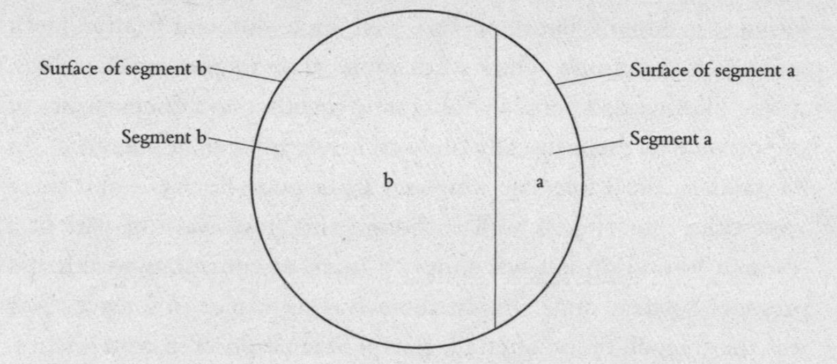

FIGURE 2.1 *Archimedes' hoax: a sphere divided into two segments*

Archimedes, it is time to reveal a secret: two of those announced discoveries were, as it were, 'poisoned'. To provide one example: Archimedes had announced his 'discovery' that, if a sphere is cut into two segments, and the ratio of the surfaces is a:b, then the ratio of the volumes is $a^2:b^2$ (see fig. 2.1).

I wish to stress that there is no doubt, on internal evidence of his own writings, that Archimedes indeed was aware, from early on, that these two claims were false. He is not trying to save face, retroactively: he really did send out 'poisoned' letters, hoping to trap his fellow mathematicians. As he puts it, he did this 'so that those who claim to discover everything, producing no proof themselves, will be confuted, in their assenting to prove the impossible'.

Archimedes, you should note, did not have a gentle character – nor did he have an earnest one. 'Playful' is one term that comes to mind, 'sly' another. It is not for nothing that historians keep debating the precise meaning of Archimedes' discoveries: he *meant* his readers to be puzzled. So, incidentally, he would have thoroughly relished the future history of his writings. That the effort to read him is so tantalising, so difficult, is precisely as Archimedes wanted.

The entire structure of scientific activity in Archimedes' time was radically different from anything we are familiar with. There were no universities, no jobs, no scientific journals. It is true that, about a century before Archimedes' death, a number of 'schools' were founded in Athens, but these, too, were quite different from modern scientific institutions. They were more akin to present-day clubs, where like-minded people could come together and discuss issues of importance to them (usually philosophical rather than scientific). In Alexandria, the Ptolemaic kings set up a huge library – and there were other libraries, as well – though this, too, was not part of a research institution but was simply a mark of enormous wealth and prestige. So that, quite simply, there was no career in science. Nor was there much glory: after all, few people could even read science. The real path to glory was – then as always in the pre-modern world – via *poetry*. If you wanted to make a name for yourself, to win some kind of eternity, you would write poems – which, after all, was what everyone read (starting, in early childhood, with the *Iliad* and the *Odyssey*, which everyone more or less knew by heart).

How would one become a mathematician? You would have to be exposed to it by chance (say, by your father, if he happened to be an astronomer . . .). And then you were hooked. This was a rare affliction. I once estimated that in the entire period of ancient mathematics – roughly from 500 BC to AD 500 – there were, perhaps, a thousand active mathematicians – one born every year, say, on average. I should make clear right now that earlier figures – such as Pythagoras and Thales – were not mathematicians at all; the name 'Pythagoras' theorem' is a late myth. Mathematics begins in the fifth century BC – the age of Pericles and the Parthenon – with authors of whom, however, very little is known. Perhaps the most important was Hippocrates of Chios (not to be confused with the doctor of the same name, from Cos). All we know of such authors derives from late quotations and commentaries. In the fourth century BC not much more is known: Archytas was Plato's friend and a great mathematician – but only a single proof survives by him. Even that does not survive from Eudoxus, later in the century; but he is mentioned twice, with admiration, by Archimedes. Apparently Archimedes considered Eudoxus to be his greatest predecessor; but the works of this predecessor are now all lost.

Not so the works of Euclid, writing, perhaps, early in the third century. They survive in plenty. But Archimedes wouldn't think very highly of them, as they consist mainly of basic mathematics. Archimedes was an advanced mathematician, writing for people who knew much more than just the contents of Euclid's *Elements*. And there must have been very few of these. I believe that Archimedes may have had an 'audience' consisting of a few dozen mathematicians at most, spread around the Mediterranean, many of them isolated in their small towns, impatiently waiting for the next delivery of letters from Alexandria (the exchange centre) – is there anything new sent out by Archimedes?

When Archimedes' introductions start out with a letter sent to an individual, this should be understood in a very literal way. These *were* private letters – sent out to people in Alexandria who had the contacts to deliver the contents further. Everything depended on this network of individuals. Archimedes keeps lamenting, in his introductions, the death of his older friend Conon (who was an important astronomer). He was the only one who could understand me! ... In most of Archimedes' letters there is a faint note of exasperation: there was no one to write to, no reader good enough. (There would be, in time: Archimedes would eventually be read by Omar Khayyam, by Leonardo da Vinci, by Galileo, by Newton; these were Archimedes' real readers and the ones through whom he has made his real impact. He must have known that he was writing for posterity.)

Many of the works are addressed to Dositheus, of whom very little is known otherwise. We do know one thing – yet again, based on the name alone. It turns out that practically everyone in Alexandria at that time who was called Dositheus was Jewish. (The name, in fact, is simply the Greek version of Matityahu, or Matthew.) This is very curious: the correspondence between Archimedes and Dositheus is the *only* one known from antiquity between a Greek and a Jew, and it is perhaps telling that the place for such cross-cultural contact is with science. In mathematics, after all, religion and nation do not matter: this, at least, has not changed.

Squaring Circles

And what mathematics it was, sent to Dositheus! First came a treatise on the *Quadrature of the Parabola.* Then two separate books on *Sphere and Cylinder.* Then a book on *Spiral Lines* (the one where the hoax was revealed). And, finally, a book on *Conoids and Spheroids.* (There might have been more: these are the five books that survive.) The five works form a certain unity, as together they constitute the cornerstone of the calculus, though this is probably not how Archimedes would have thought of them. To him, they were all variations on squaring the circle. That is: time and again, Archimedes takes an object bounded by curved lines and equates it with a much simpler object, preferably bounded by straight lines. Apparently this task – squaring, or measuring, the circle – was, for Greek mathematicians, the Holy Grail of their science.

The very idea of measurement depends on the notion of the straight line. It is not for nothing that we measure with *rulers.* To measure is to find some measuring tool and then to apply it successively to the object measured. Suppose we want to measure a straight line. For instance, suppose we want to measure your height – which is really saying that we want to measure the straight line reaching from the floor to the top of your head. Then what we do is take a line the length of a centimetre and apply it successively, well over a hundred times though probably less than two hundred times, to measure your height. Since this is very tiresome, we have pre-marked measuring tapes that save us the trouble of actually applying the length successively, but at the conceptual level successive application is precisely what takes place.

With an area instead of a length, we do the same but now take not a straight line as our measuring unit but instead a square, which we apply successively: this is why floor plans are literally measured by square feet. Volumes, once again, are measured by cubes. Of course, not all objects come pre-packaged in squared or cubed units. However,

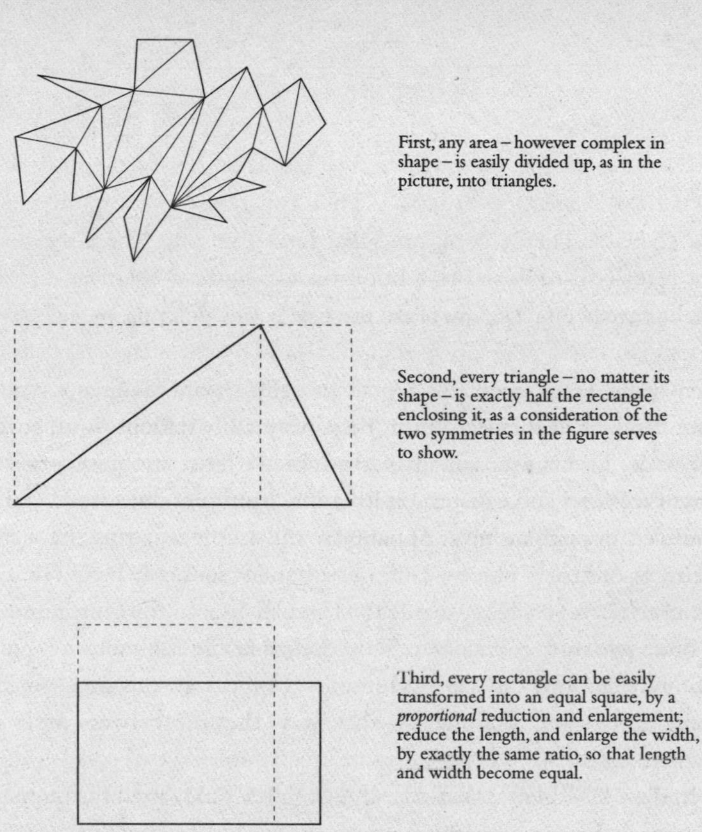

FIGURE 2.2 *How to measure an area bounded by straight lines*

Greek mathematicians from very early on came up with three important discoveries (see fig. 2.2):

- Every area bound by straight lines can be divided up into triangles.
- Every triangle can be made equal to half a rectangle.
- Every rectangle can be made equal to a square.

The combination of these three facts means that it is possible to measure any area bounded by straight lines as a sum of squares. The same, analogously, holds for solids divided into pyramids which are

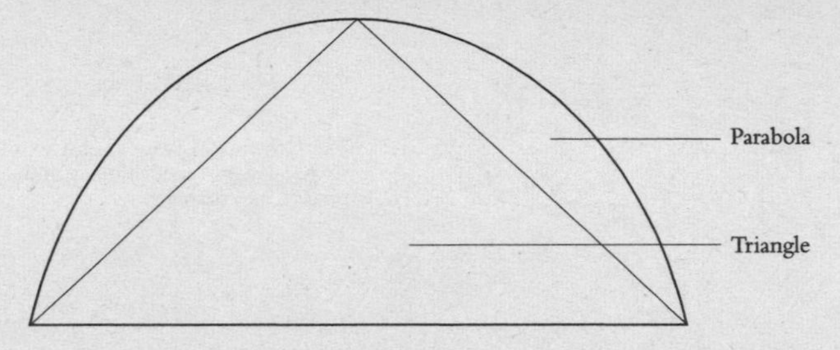

FIGURE 2.3 *The area of the parabola is four-thirds the triangle*

then made equal to cubes. It is all straightforward. Take any object bounded by straight lines. It can be conceptually difficult – a Rubik's cube or a many-spangled snowflake – but its measurement always follows the same principle and is truly straightforward. Take, however, instead, an object as apparently simple as a baseball – just the most ordinary sphere – and measurement suddenly breaks down, because it is impossible to divide the baseball up into any finite number of finite pyramids or triangles. The baseball has an infinitely complex, infinitely smooth surface. Archimedes would measure such objects again and again, pushing in this way the most basic tools of mathematics.

In the *Quadrature of the Parabola* Archimedes measured the segment of a parabola: it is four-thirds times the triangle it encloses (see fig. 2.3) – a very striking measurement, given that the parabola is a curved line, so this is rather like squaring a circle. He also, in the same treatise, introduced a certain daring thought experiment: to conceive of a geometrical object as if it were composed of physical slices hung on a balance.

The two books on *Sphere and Cylinder* directly approach the volume of the sphere. It turns out it is exactly two-thirds the cylinder enclosing it. What is its surface? It turns out it is exactly four times its greatest circle (see fig. 2.4). This recalcitrant object – the sphere – turns out to obey some very precise rules. In the second book remarkable tasks are achieved: such as, for instance, finding the ratio between spherical segments (which was the substance of the hoax mentioned above).

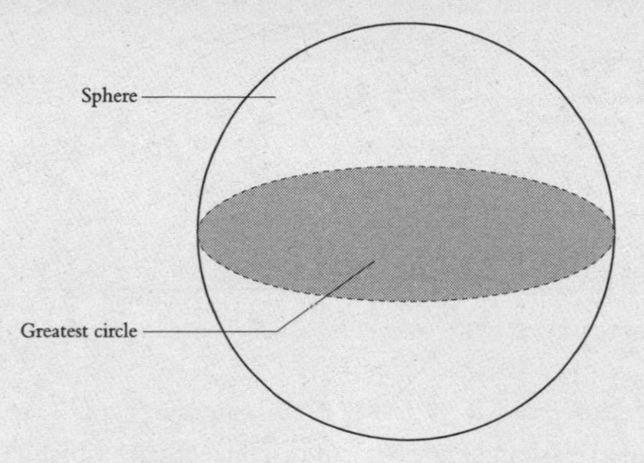

FIGURE 2.4 *The surface of the sphere is four times the area of its greatest circle*

In both *Spiral Lines* and *Conoids and Spheroids* Archimedes is not content to measure known objects. Instead he invents a new curved object – a complex, counter-intuitive object – and then measures it. The spiral line – invented by Archimedes – turns out to enclose exactly one-third the area enclosed by the circle surrounding it (see fig. 2.5). As for conoids (which are hyperbolas or parabolas turned around so as to enclose space) or spheroids (which are ellipses turned around in similar fashion) – these have more complex measurements, which, however, are all obtained, with precision, by Archimedes (see figs. 2.6, 2.7).

This is a major feature of all these works: Archimedes starts out by promising to make some incredible measurement, and you expect him to fudge it somehow, to cut corners (how else can you *square the circle*?) And then he begins to surprise you. He accumulates results of no obvious relevance – some proportions between this and that line; some special constructions of no direct connection to the problem at hand. And then – about midway through the treatise – he lets you see how all the results build together and, 'By God!' you exclaim, 'he is actually going to prove this precisely, no fudges made!'

Each of these works was of a completely different order of

FIGURE 2.5 *The area of the circle is three times the area enclosed by the spiral*

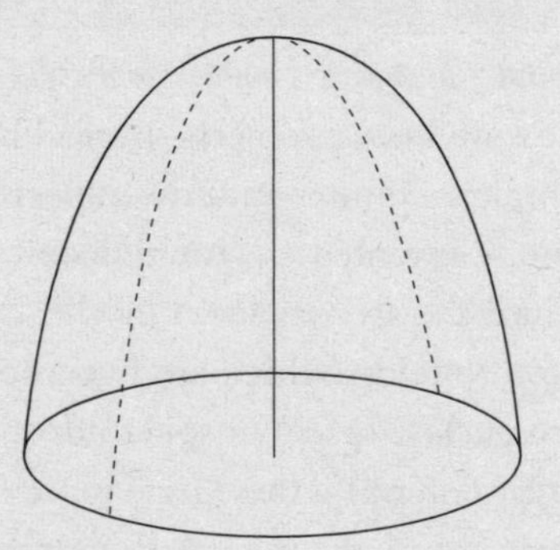

FIGURE 2.6 *A conoid is a solid created by rotating a parabola or a hyperbola on its axis*

originality and brilliance from anything ever seen before. In all of them Archimedes was furthering the mathematics of infinity.

Imaginary Dialogues

In his measurements Archimedes adopts a surprising, circuitous route – always his favourite way of approaching things. The general plan is as

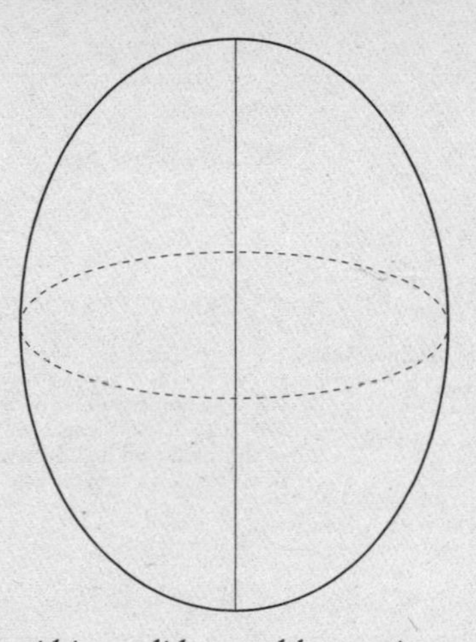

FIGURE 2.7 *A spheroid is a solid created by rotating an ellipse on its axis*

follows: apply a combination of 'indirect proof' and 'potential infinity'.

Both indirect proof and potential infinity are best considered as imaginary dialogues. That of indirect proof is easier to understand – you have probably engaged in some version of it yourself. You try to convince someone of the truth of your position. Let us say, for instance, that you want to convince your interlocutor that, when you draw a straight line joining two points on the circumference of a circle, all the points on this straight line must fall *inside* the circle. Everything you tell him about this line fails to persuade him. And so you resort to indirect proof. You assume the opposite of the truth, as if pretending to agree with your interlocutor.

'Let us assume that some point E falls outside the circle,' you concede (see fig. 2.8). And now you follow the logic of this situation, until you draw the following conclusion: the line DZ is both smaller than DE and bigger than it. But a line cannot at the same time be both smaller and greater than the same given line. 'See' – you now turn to your imaginary interlocutor – 'I have conceded your claim, but the result was an absurdity; therefore this claim of yours must be false. I have now proved this *indirectly*.' This type of argument is one of the hallmarks of Greek mathematics.

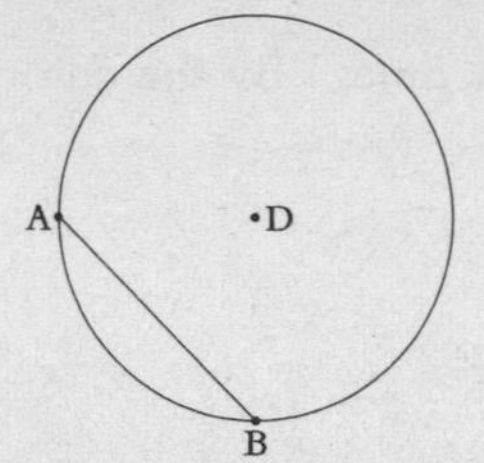

The line AB must never get out of the circle.

Imagine it does, as the 'line' AEB.

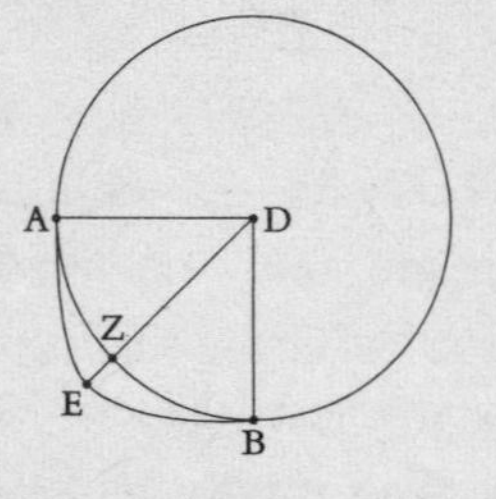

DE is greater than DZ, because it contains it: **DE > DZ**. DZ is equal to DB (both are radii of the circle), while DB, in turn, is greater than DE. (This is because in a triangle such as

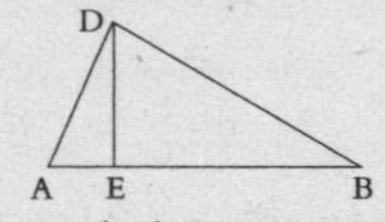

the external side DB is greater than the internal line DE.) As a consequence, DZ is greater than DE: **DZ > DE**.

Both DZ > DE and DE > DZ ⟶ Contradiction!

FIGURE 2.8 *Indirect proof: why does a line never get out of its circle?*

Potential infinity was not invented by Archimedes, but he made it his own, in a series of original applications of it. You remember the fundamental problem with measuring a curved object: it could not be divided up fully into triangles; with any finite number of triangles in it, there is always some piece of the curved object 'left out'. Now let us concentrate on the size of this piece that is left out. What Archimedes does is develop a certain mechanism, capable of indefinite extension, of packing in triangles (or their like) into the curved object. This is best seen, once again, as an imaginary dialogue between Archimedes and his critic.

Let us say he has packed the curved object in a certain way, so that a certain area has been left out, an area greater than the size of a grain of sand.

A critic comes along and points out that there is still a difference the size of a grain of sand.

'Is that right?' exclaims Archimedes. 'All right then, I shall apply my mechanism successively several more times.' By the end of this operation the area left out is now smaller than the grain of sand.

'Wait a minute,' says the critic, not yet satisfied. 'The area left out is still greater than a hair's width.'

Archimedes, unfazed, goes on and applies the mechanism once again, with the area left out becoming smaller than the hair's width.

'No, no!' the critic squabbles again; 'the area left out is still bigger than an atom.'

The critic may think he has had the last word, but Archimedes just goes on applying his mechanism. 'See,' he returns now to the critic: 'the area left out is now even smaller than the atom' – and so it goes on, the difference always becoming smaller than any given magnitude mentioned by the critic.

This dialogue could go on *indefinitely*. This is what philosophers refer to as *potential infinity*. We never go as far as infinity itself in this argument (there is no mention, at any point, of an area which is *infinitesimally* small, merely of areas that are *very, indefinitely* small). But we allow ourselves to go on *indefinitely*. And this, taken together with indirect proof, allows Archimedes to measure the most incredible objects.

Squaring the Parabola

Three times in his career Archimedes proved that the parabolic segment – a certain curved object – is exactly four-thirds the triangle it encloses. This was his favourite measurement. Later on we shall see his most spectacular measurement, which transcends geometry itself. But before we can follow such flights of imagination we must first acquaint ourselves with Archimedes' geometrical method itself – based throughout on the combination of indirect proof and potential infinity. It is an extraordinarily subtle argument, one that even professional mathematicians have a hard time unravelling. It is like an

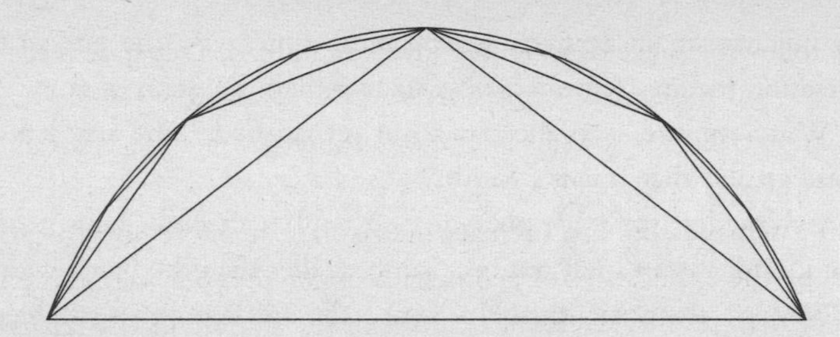

FIGURE 2.9-1 *The parabola encloses a jumble of triangles. This can be made to approach the parabola as closely as we wish. We assume its difference from the parabola is less than a grain of sand.*

affirmation based on double double negation. And this is how it works.

Since what we are going to prove is that the area of the curve is four-thirds the triangle, how shall we start? By assuming, of course, that the area of the curve is *not* four-thirds the triangle! This, after all, is how indirect proof works. Let us assume that the curved area is greater than four-thirds the triangle, by a certain amount:

1. The curve is greater than four-thirds the triangle, by a certain amount. Let us say, it is greater by a grain of sand.

For exactly such occasions, Archimedes has a special mechanism up his sleeve. He is now going to fill up the curve with triangles so that the difference between the triangles and the curve is going to be *smaller* than the grain of sand!

We therefore now have two objects side by side. One is the curve. The other is the product of Archimedes' mechanism – a complex jumble of triangles, whose difference from the curve is known to be *smaller* than a grain of sand:

2. The curve, with a grain of sand removed, is smaller than the jumble of triangles (see fig. 2.9-1).

At this point Archimedes leaves aside the results obtained so far.

The following piece of reasoning involves, instead, a separate piece of geometrical ingenuity. Remember that the jumble of triangles is an object bounded by straight lines. Four-thirds the enclosed triangle is also an object bounded by straight lines, i.e. both are objects that can be precisely measured by ordinary means. It is therefore not a surprise that, by the application of geometrical ingenuity, one can come up with a definite measurement comparing the jumble of the triangles and four-thirds the enclosed triangle. What Archimedes would come up with – applying his geometrical ingenuity – is as follows:

3. The jumble of triangles is smaller than four-thirds the enclosed triangle (see fig. 2.9-2).

Now, recall result 1. This was: 'The curve is greater than four-thirds the triangle, by a grain of sand.' Or, put differently:

4. The curve, with a grain of sand removed, is equal to four-thirds the triangle.

Put this alongside result 2: 'The curve, with a grain of sand removed, is smaller than the jumble of triangles.'

The same object is *equal* to four-thirds the triangle, but it is *smaller* than the jumble of triangles; in other words, the jumble of triangles is the greater – it is greater than four-thirds the triangle, which we may put as:

5. The jumble of triangles is greater than four-thirds the enclosed triangle.

Which makes no sense if we put it side by side with result 3: 'The jumble of triangles is smaller than four-thirds the enclosed triangle.'

Results 5 and 3 directly contradict each other. There is no way to reconcile them. The jumble of triangles cannot be both smaller and greater than four-thirds the enclosed triangle. In other words, we are left with only one option: concluding that our original assumption was wrong. The curve is *not different from* four-thirds the enclosed triangle. The curve *is* therefore four-thirds the enclosed triangle.

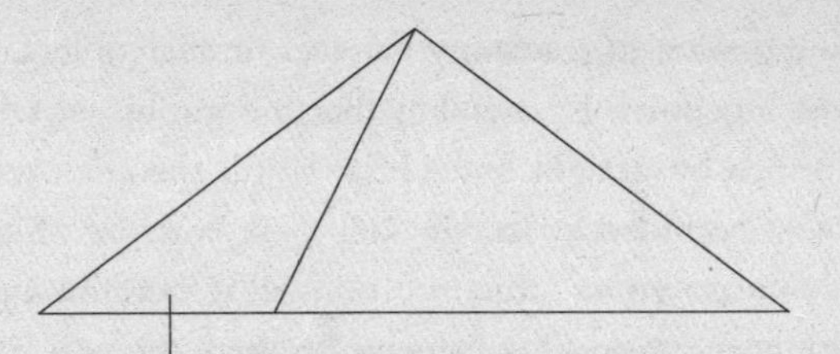

One-third the triangle + the triangle =

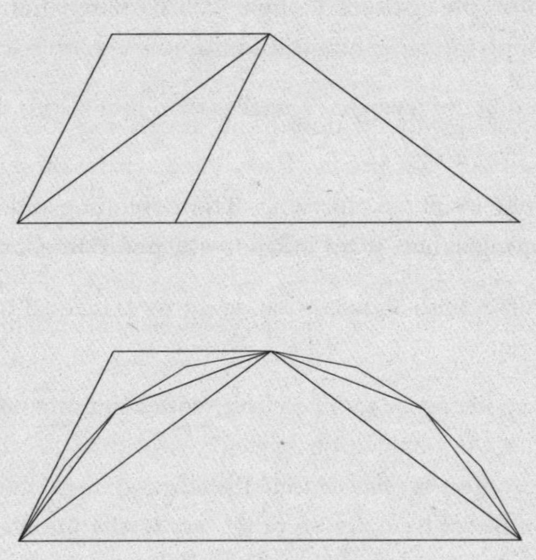

The jumble of triangles is smaller than four-thirds the enclosed triangle.

FIGURE 2.9-2

The result is therefore obtained. Indirect proof and potential infinity together have brought us there.

Beyond Potential Infinity

Now let us go back to put this in historical context. In the seventeenth century mathematicians found a way to apply this technique of Archimedes in a more general fashion (so that, instead of finding, ingeniously, this or that strategy for this or that object, one would have a general recipe for measuring all curves). This was the calculus, which, as mentioned above, is the foundation of modern science. The persons most directly responsible for this were Newton and Leibniz, and if you wish to know which of the two deserves more credit, you are not alone: the battle for priority between Newton and Leibniz was the most famous – as well as the ugliest – in the history of science. (Most scholars today think it should be considered an honourable draw.) Both, in a sense, followed Archimedes. More than this: both Newton and Leibniz managed to bring the calculus to a great height – on shaky foundations. The underlying logic of handling potential infinities was not clearly worked out by those inventors of the calculus. It was put in order only at the beginning of the nineteenth century, especially by the French mathematician Cauchy – who essentially reverted to the Archimedes method of implicit dialogue ('You find me an area X – I'll find you a smaller difference . . .'). In every step along the way, our calculus, as well as our understanding of potential infinity, is Archimedean. So much for potential infinity. As for *actual* infinity – where one contemplates an actual infinite set of objects – it was not mastered at all by mathematicians such as Newton and Leibniz, and was put in order (if it can be called order) only in the late nineteenth century, beginning with authors such as Cantor.

And here comes the shocking surprise. In 2001 it was discovered for the first time – against all expectations – that Archimedes knew of *actual* infinity and used it in his mathematics. This was discovered through the Palimpsest and is, no doubt, the most important discovery made through its reappearance.

Proofs and Physics

The new discovery was made by reading a passage of Archimedes' *Method* that had never been read before. This work, the most fascinating of all works by Archimedes, survives in the Palimpsest alone. And it is most fascinating because here more than anywhere else Archimedes brings together his *two* interests: the mathematics of infinity, which we have seen already, and the combination of mathematics and physics, of statements of pure geometry with those about the physical world. It all comes out of the balance. Archimedes was the first to prove, mathematically, the law of the balance: objects balance when their weights are exactly reciprocal to their distances from the fulcrum. In the *Method* he pushes forward a surprising technique: take geometrical objects and produce the thought experiment where they are arranged on a balance. He then uses their weights (that is, lengths and areas) as well as distances from a centre, to measure some purely geometrical properties. The law of the balance becomes a tool of geometry instead of physics.

This work was not among the series sent to Dositheus. In fact this may be because Archimedes valued it especially highly: it was sent to the most influential intellectual of Archimedes' time, Eratosthenes. This polymath wrote on anything from Homer to astronomy, from prime numbers to Plato. As a result he was nicknamed 'Beta', as being the number two on everything ... Archimedes, who clearly saw himself as the number one in his own field, approaches Eratosthenes with great apparent respect, but he almost seems to be teasing him – as if saying 'See if you can catch me!' The work is the most fascinating by Archimedes, partly because it is the most enigmatic. Archimedes suggests that he has discovered a method of finding mathematical results which is very powerful and yet does not quite constitute a proof. But he never explains what this method actually is or how it falls short of actual proof. He leaves this as a kind of enigma, to be worked out from the text by the reader himself – first Eratosthenes and then, since the discovery of the *Method* in the twentieth century, by every historian of ancient mathematics. Everyone has a theory about the *Method*. We shall return to this enigma – perhaps to understand it better, based on the new readings of the Palimpsest.

Of course, Archimedes' claim to be the founder of mathematical physics does not rest on the *Method* alone. Of his studies in this field, two major works are still extant: *Balancing Planes* and *On Floating Bodies*. In *Balancing Planes*, which we will examine later, Archimedes finds the centre of gravity of a triangle, one of the key results of the science of statics. *On Floating Bodies* sets the stage for another science, that of hydrostatics. This work provided the foundation for Vitruvius' nice but silly story about Archimedes' splashing in the bath. He may have splashed, he may have run naked; but he certainly did not cry *Eureka* over such a trivial observation as 'bigger things make bigger splashes'. No: the deduction in *On Floating Bodies* is much more subtle and sophisticated. Here is how it works:

In a stable body of liquid, each column of equal volume must also have equal weight – otherwise liquid would flow from the heavier to the lighter (this is why the face of the sea is *even*). The same must hold true even if a solid body is immersed within such a column of liquid. In other words, if we have a column of liquid with a solid body immersed in it, the aggregate weight of the liquid and the body must be equal to that of a column of liquid of the same volume. It follows that the solid body must lose some of its weight – and a complex calculation that Archimedes follows through shows that it must lose a weight equal to the volume of water it has displaced.

This explains why we feel lighter in the bath; indeed it tells us precisely by how much we *should* feel lighter in the bath. Now that's something to cry *eureka* about! Because, you see, by the power of pure thought alone, Archimedes is capable of saying what must happen in the physical world! This power of mind over matter is what is so fascinating about Archimedean science – what Galileo and Newton tried to imitate – and, incredibly, succeeded in imitating. So that, finally, Newton discovered, by the power of pure thought – as well as by the calculus – *how the planets must move*. And, with this Archimedean achievement, Newton set the stage for all of later science.

Puzzles and Numbers

Newtonian science was sober-minded; Archimedes' science was not. Archimedes was famous for hoaxes, enigmas, circuitous routes. These were not some external features of his writings: they characterised his scientific personality. Science is not – mathematics is not – dry and impersonal. It is where one's imagination is allowed to roam freely. And so, Archimedes' imagination roamed and he came up with a child's play called the Stomachion, or Bellyache (from the difficulty of solving it): a tangram puzzle of fourteen pieces, made to form a square. And Archimedes wondered: what was the underlying mathematics of this puzzle?

This, in fact, was a puzzle to us modern scholars, as well. Since 1906 we have known that Archimedes wrote on this Stomachion puzzle. But just what was he trying to do? We had available to us only a single bifolio of the Palimpsest – one of the worst preserved. Heiberg had made little sense of the Greek and none of the mathematics. Digital technology, finally, allowed us to make further readings and, in 2003, I was finally able to offer an interpretation of the Stomachion – the first ever offered in modern times. I argue that Archimedes was trying to do the following: to calculate how many ways one can form the square given the original fourteen pieces. There is more than a single way, as figure 2.10 illustrates. In point of fact, there are 17,152 distinct solutions.

The most striking thing about this interpretation is not the very big number itself but something else: if true (and most historians think I am likely to be right), then this would make Archimedes the first author, ever, on *combinatorics* – the field of mathematics calculating the number of possible solutions to a given problem. This, then, was the second important discovery made through the Archimedes Palimpsest.

The field of combinatorics is at the heart of modern computer sciences, but it had no such application in Archimedes' own time and is very different in character from the kind of geometrical study we

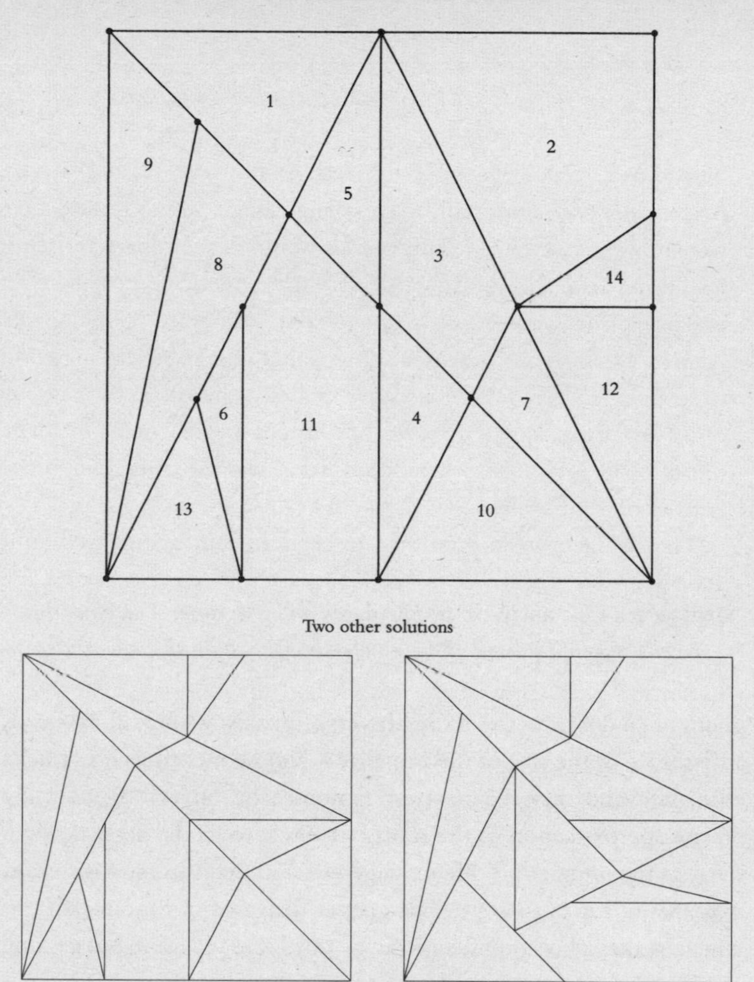

FIGURE 2.10 *The Stomachion*

see so often in Greek mathematics. Indeed, the Stomachion appears like a pure flight of fancy. You look for a number because it is there. And along the way you generate a fantastic array of complicated calculations. Archimedes, after all, was a master of this game, this hunt for big numbers and surprising combinations. There is a treatise of his (extant) called the *Sand-Reckoner,* in which he calculates how many

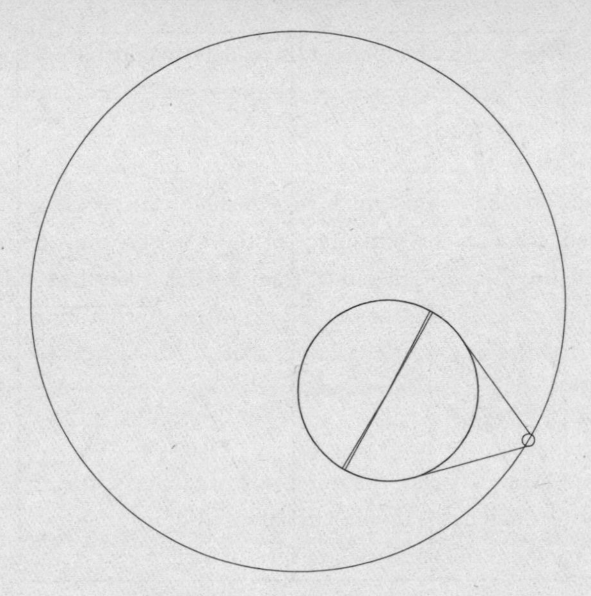

FIGURE 2.11 *A ninety-six-sided polygon within a circle. The inner circle shows a magnified detail of the ninety-six-gon within the outer circle.*

grains of sand it takes to fill the universe (for this, you recall, he needs an estimate of the size of the universe – and he mentions his father's estimate). And then again, most famously, he offers a fantastically precise approximation of the ratio of a circle to its diameter (known today as the number pi). He managed to find that this ratio is smaller than that of 14688 to $4673\frac{1}{2}$, but greater than that of 6336 to $2017\frac{1}{4}$ – which he then also simplified (losing a tiny bit in precision but gaining much more in clarity) to the ratio being smaller than three and a seventh, and greater than three and ten-seventy-oneths(!). This amazing calculation is based on a method not unlike that of the treatment of potentially infinite series, only that, in the case of the circumference of the circle, precise calculation is impossible and so approximation works best. So that Archimedes calculates not the circumference of a circle but that of a polygon with ninety-six sides – which, to sight, is nearly the same (see fig. 2.11).

Perhaps the most strikingly playful calculation made by Archimedes is that of the cattle of Helios. His readers would have known the context from their memories of Homer's *Odyssey*. In book twelve Odysseus' crew reaches the island of Thrinacia, sacred to Helios. Against Odysseus' advice his crew members are tempted to slaughter the cattle of Helios, on which they feast lavishly – for seven days! And then, through the remainder of the *Odyssey*, they are horribly punished for this transgression. Tradition has identified this island with Sicily, so that the story could be turned into a kind of poetic tribute to Sicily's power, a warning that it should not be interfered with. Archimedes puts this as yet another riddle, a calculatory puzzle couched in a poem:

> Measure for me, friend, the multitude of Helios' cattle,
> Possessing diligence – if you partake of wisdom:
> How many did once graze the plains of Sicily,
> The Island Thrinacian divided in four herds,
> In colour varied . . .
> [The text goes on for about three pages, with many mathematical constraints such as, for instance:]
> . . . The white bulls
> Were of the black a half and then a third
> And then the whole of yellows, friend, do know this . . .

In short, Archimedes constructs an arithmetical problem with eight unknowns (there are four herds, black, white, yellow and many-spangled, each divided into both bulls and cows), with seven equations (e.g. the one above: [white bulls] = ⅚ [black bulls] + [yellow bulls]) and two extra – complex conditions where the solutions must obviously be in integer numbers (there are no half-cows). To try to solve this problem, it turns out, is a transgression as fateful as was the original slaughter. Do it at your peril: modern mathematicians have proved that the smallest solution involves a number written out in 206,456 digits.

This was a game. For, you see, the presentation above – with the short, metrical lines – was not whimsical on my part. *Archimedes wrote out this problem in verse.* A poet-mathematician! – the thought seems to us absurd, but it was natural for Archimedes, whose entire science was based on a sense of play and beauty, on hidden meanings. In this case, no doubt, the hidden meanings were, among other things, political: Archimedes was trying to suggest that one should not interfere with Sicily. Many did, in his time, and he did his best to stop them. And here, finally, we return to the historical facts of Archimedes' life.

Death and Afterlife

Syracuse was the leading city of Sicily – the pivot between eastern and western Mediterranean. Previous invaders had already tried to take it, most famously Athens in the year 415 BC – when it tried to force the outcome of the Peloponnesian War by gaining the riches of Sicily. The crashing failure of that expedition marked the end of the Athenian Empire.

So it was with some realistic hope that the Syracusans were waiting, in 214, for the Romans to come. For a generation now Syracuse, nominally free, had been tightly enmeshed within the Roman sphere of influence. Undoubtedly Archimedes – like most of his fellow citizens – was eager to shake off this indirect Roman control. Hannibal's recent victories over the Romans appeared to make this finally possible. Syracuse openly sided with the Carthaginians. Unless the Romans could contain and reduce this city, their own fate would be sealed. For, through Sicily, Hannibal would be resupplied while Roman manpower had not yet recovered from its recent catastrophe. The Romans, their power so depleted, could not withstand the siege for years on end. So the fate of the Mediterranean rested on this question: could Syracuse take it for long enough?

The previous century had seen a military revolution. From the wars of hoplites clashing on the battlefield a new kind of warfare had evolved – that of the siege. In the ancient world's version of an arms race all cities were building up their walls while, at the same time, all military powers were building up their arsenals of catapults – the machines that drove the military revolution. In principle a catapult is no more than a huge spring that, once released, serves to propel a rock to smash into walls or people. It can be surprisingly effective, knocking down, in time, some very sturdy defences. But then again one needs to get the catapult within range of the walls – where it will be within range of the catapults from inside – and so, on with the arms race.

The Romans fully expected the Syracusans to spring rocks on them. Yet they were in for a surprise. I now quote from Polybius, a very sober historian who wrote not long after the events described here – the best source we have for Archimedes' life. Here is the surprise sprung by Syracuse on its invaders:

> But Archimedes, who had prepared machines constructed to carry to any distance, so damaged the assailants at long range, as they sailed up [the first attempt was by sea] with his more powerful catapults as to throw them into much difficulty and distress; and as soon as these machines shot too high he continued using smaller and smaller ones as the range became shorter and, finally, so thoroughly shook their courage that he put a complete stop to their advance . . . [The Romans gave up the assault, and so Polybius sums up:] Such a great and marvellous thing does the genius of one man show itself to be . . . The Romans, strong as they were both by sea and land, had every hope of capturing the town at once if one old man of Syracuse were removed; but as long as he was present, they did not venture even to attempt to attack . . .

What did Archimedes do? After all, catapults were well known before him. What seems to have taken the Romans completely off balance was the careful sighting and ranging of the catapults. There were no 'blind spots', a crucial consideration; for otherwise one could find those spots and hop for safety from one spot to another, largely disabling the scheme of defence.

How to avoid blind spots and to sight your catapults? This is a formidable problem, not at all capable of solution by means of simple trial and error. For one had to have some principle of *constructing a catapult to order* – that is, one which, positioned at a given point, would cover a precise range.

At the most basic, this involves a deep problem of geometry. The propulsive power of a catapult is roughly equivalent to its mass (which determines the physical force it may exert). This, in turn, is roughly equivalent to its volume. Now, how do we measure volumes? Just as we do surfaces: by multiplying the dimensions (two in the case of surfaces, three in the case of volumes). Since a solid has three dimensions, its volume is equivalent to the cubic power of its linear dimension. So let us say that you have a catapult whose length is a yard, and you wish to transform it into another catapult twice as powerful. Making it two yards long would obviously be wrong: a two-yard-long catapult would be not twice as powerful but eight times more powerful. How to get a catapult twice as powerful, then? For this, we must find the *cubic root of two* (which is roughly 1.26) and then extend the length (and all other linear measurements) by that ratio. The finding of cubic roots is not an easy task at all; in fact it calls for very powerful mathematical techniques. Greek mathematicians had already tackled the problem, but there were few solutions allowing any practical applications. None is known in Archimedes' name, but there is no doubt that he had found such a technique and applied it in the year 214.

But I suspect more than this. Here is a pure flight of fancy on my part. After all, since Archimedes could tell *where a missile would land* – that is, follow in his imagination the curve traced by that missile – would he not then have concentrated his attention on the problem of *representing projectile motion as a geometrical curve*? Would he not have found the curve – his beloved parabola – and used it so as to place his catapults in position? For, after all, Archimedes' pupils Galileo and Newton did, basing their ideas on mathematical techniques not so different from those used by Archimedes himself. Galileo traced the motions of projectiles, Newton, those of planets, using precisely those parabolas. Archimedes would have had interesting problems to ponder, surely, constructing those machines!

And so legend has it: picture Archimedes in the year 212 BC, pondering his problems. The Roman siege is nearly defeated, Archimedes' genius triumphing over Roman power. Complacency has set in. The Syracusans are celebrating a festival, a deserter informs the Romans that the sentries, drunk, have deserted their posts. The Roman general Marcellus quickly dispatches a group of soldiers to occupy positions on the wall and, as ever in this kind of warfare, once a breach is made the game is up. Soon the city is overtaken by the Romans. They have little reason to be merciful: Syracuse has been counting on Rome's downfall, and now Rome thoroughly relishes the reversal of its fortune. The looting is unprecedented in scale, even for the Romans – who now take away everything that can be removed.

We are told that the booty included a huge planetarium, a marvel of science, produced by Archimedes himself. We are also told that Marcellus wished to capture and bring home Archimedes in person, but – as has always happened in history – with the pillage came a spree of senseless murder. The legend is famous, reported by Plutarch:

> He was by himself, working out some problem with the aid of a diagram, and having fixed his thoughts and his eyes as well upon the matter of his study, he was not aware of the incursion of the Romans or of the capture of the city. Suddenly a soldier came upon him and ordered him to go with him to Marcellus. This Archimedes refused to do until he had worked out his problem and established its demonstration, whereupon the soldier flew into a passion, drew his sword, and killed him.

So much for the legend. (Plutarch himself reviews several other alternatives, and the truth is likely be different still.) But it is an appropriate legend. Several ignorant hands nearly brought an end to Archimedes' heritage by destroying a scientific legacy that they did not understand. Yet Archimedes survived.

For we may conclude with sober historical fact, instead of legend. Let us follow Cicero in the year 75 BC. Archimedes has been dead for 137 years. Sicily is a Roman province, part of a Mediterranean that has been thoroughly subdued. Cicero himself is a quaestor, a high official, on the island. He is also a cultivated man, with deep respect for the Greek scientific heritage. He knows about the old tomb of Archimedes and is capable of finding it again, despite its having been lost for all those years. And on the tomb the old engraving (requested by Archimedes himself) is still there: a sphere, and a cylinder exactly enclosing it.

Archimedes did prove that the first was always two-thirds the second – a masterpiece of reasoning that got him as close to squaring the circle as is humanly possible. The diagram on this tomb was immortal. Archimedes did find the first deep, revolutionary truths. In time, they would give rise to our science. But first, his works had to survive – to cross the seas of history so that, on the other shore, modern science could be born.

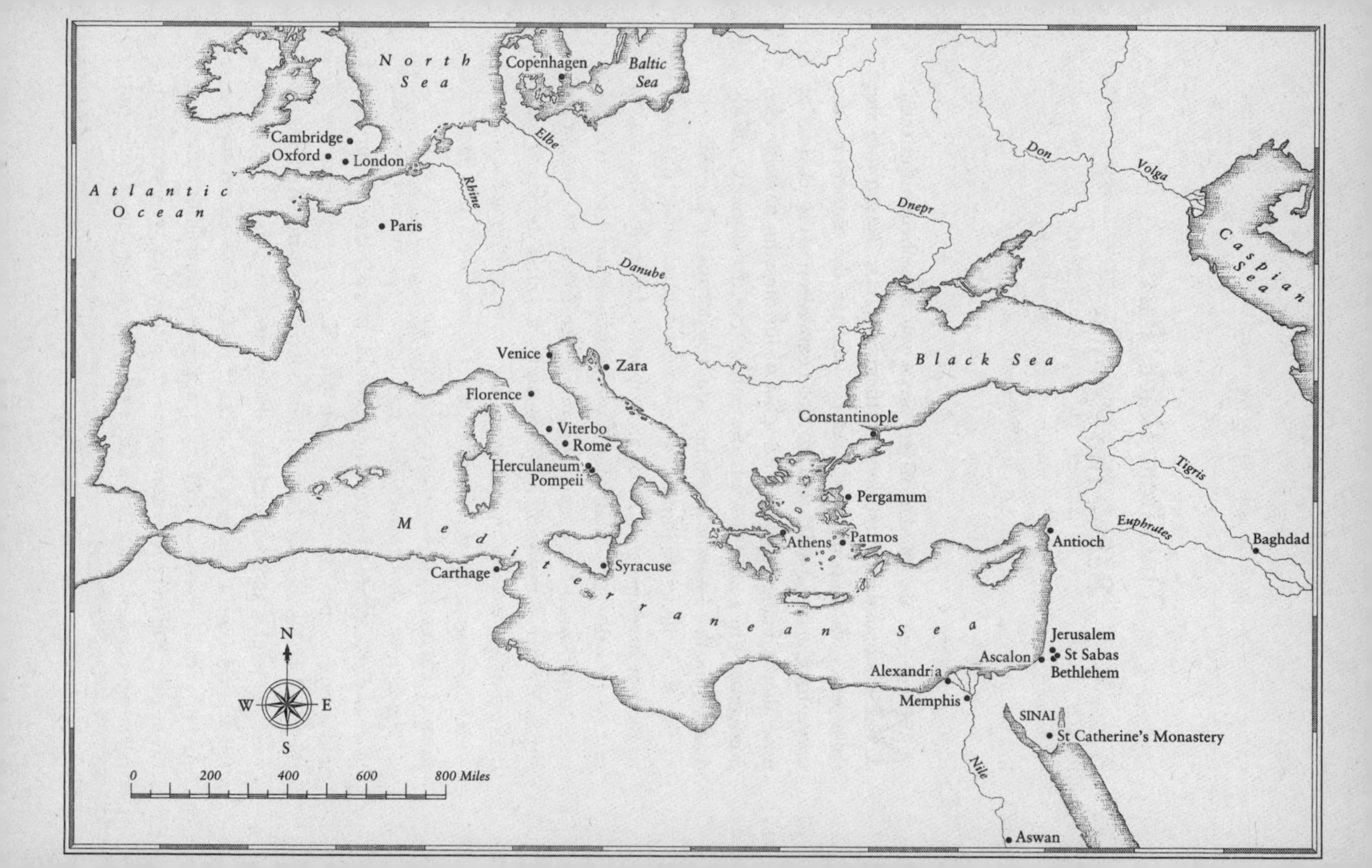
North Sea
Copenhagen
Baltic Sea
Cambridge
Oxford
London
Atlantic Ocean
Paris
Elbe
Rhine
Danube
Dnepr
Don
Volga
Caspian Sea
Black Sea
Venice
Zara
Florence
Viterbo
Rome
Herculaneum
Pompeii
Constantinople
Pergamum
Athens
Patmos
Antioch
Tigris
Euphrates
Baghdad
Carthage
Syracuse
Mediterranean Sea
Jerusalem
St Sabas
Bethlehem
Ascalon
Alexandria
Memphis
SINAI
St Catherine's Monastery
Nile
Aswan
N
E
S
W
0
200
400
600
800 Miles

3

The Great Race, Part 1
Before the Palimpsest

Mr B sent me another letter, but it wasn't a cheque this time. It contained transcripts of the court case concerning the Palimpsest, which continued after the sale. In the transcripts, the lawyer for Christie's said that plans for an exhibition of the manuscript were already being explored through a major museum in Baltimore. Sometimes I'm a little slow on the uptake, but it did pretty quickly occur to me that I was the guy who would be putting on an exhibition of the Archimedes Palimpsest in the near future. Since the book would not have made much of an exhibition by itself, I decided to make a film that explained why it was so important. I got in touch with John Dean, a film-maker and now a dear friend. He bought the airplane tickets – thankfully to Sicily and not Samos (he knew more than I did) and we flew around the Mediterranean making the movie, with John singing and making friends all the way. We had to pack the story of 2,200 years into two weeks of filming.

The film was about a race. The race lasted for centuries and took place over the entire Mediterranean world. It was a race for survival, and it was an epic. Archimedes rode on a donkey – the concern of the scholar and the care of the scribe. Arrayed against Archimedes were the mighty thoroughbreds of destruction: war, indifference and the second law of thermodynamics. If his works were to survive, Archimedes had to stay ahead of his opposition throughout the race; his treatises had to be rewritten more times than they were destroyed. All ancient authors were in the same race and facing similar odds. But for most of them, thanks to the printing press of Johannes Gutenberg, the race was effectively over by the end of the sixteenth century. From 1454 onwards, these authors dismounted from their donkeys and climbed on to Pegasus, the winged horse. Even destruction's thoroughbreds found it difficult to overtake the printing press. But Gutenberg's invention was still 1,666 years away when Archimedes died. By a series of truly fantastic circumstances, Archimedes' race is not over even in the twenty-first century, and the final lap is being conducted in the New World.

A Letter is Written

The soccer ball kicked by Italy – that's how you might think of it. But it isn't a sphere; it's a triangle. And that's how the ancients thought of the island of Sicily. John Dean and I landed in Palermo, which is on the western angle of the triangle, and we drove through its centre at Piazza Armerina, then down towards the south-east angle, leaving Mount Etna on our left. We arrived at Archimedes' home town, Syracuse. John and I stayed in Winston Churchill's favourite hotel, but we walked the streets that Archimedes trod, sat in the theatre where he watched plays, visited the altar at which he worshipped, and followed the city walls that he defended. High above the city, on the Epipolae Plain, still stand the impressive remains of the Euryalus fortress. In April 1999 it looked stunning, its white ramparts emerging from a sea of wild flowers. The view was magnificent, and we could see the port below us, to the east.

From Syracuse, before the Second Punic War, Archimedes had written a letter to a friend. The letter began:

> Archimedes to Eratosthenes: greetings! Since I know you are diligent, an excellent teacher of philosophy, and greatly interested in any mathematical investigation that may come your way, I thought it might be appropriate to write down and set

> forth for you a certain special method . . . I presume there will be some among the present as well as future generations who by means of the method here explained will be enabled to find other theorems which have not yet fallen to our share.

It is easy to accept recorded history as a full account of the past. It isn't, and if we think of it this way, we not only misunderstand what history is but also miss marvelling at what it is that we know. Nothing is inevitable about the fact that we know that a great man in the third century BC wrote a private letter to a friend; it is absolutely extraordinary that we know this. Amazingly, we also know a lot of what he wrote in the letter, and even what it looked like.

The letter was made of papyrus sheets and wrapped around a wooden core. In other words, it was a roll. Papyrus is a fibrous plant that used to grow plentifully in the Nile delta, and papyrus rolls were the stationery of choice in the ancient Mediterranean. Strips taken from the lower stem of the plant were laid down parallel, and slightly overlapping each other. Then another set of strips was laid down at right angles to the first. The two layers were bashed together with a mallet and they would stick together to make an excellent writing surface. Sections could be glued together to make rolls of different lengths. The rolls were made in Egypt, and distributed throughout the ancient world from Alexandria, the greatest trading port of the ancient world. To write on the roll, Archimedes used a reed pen and wrote on just one side of the sheet – the side on which the papyrus leaves were laid horizontally. He wrote in narrow columns of capital letters, not down the length of the roll but down its width. He did not leave spaces between his words, and there was virtually no punctuation as we understand it. His diagrams, which he regarded as integral to his text, were placed within the columns of his text, following the text to which they referred.

Once he had finished his letter Archimedes took it to the port and arranged for it to be shipped to its destination. He was sending his roll on a perilous sea voyage, right back to where it had come from –

Alexandria. If he kept a copy of what he sent – and this was standard practice – then no trace of that copy survives. Perhaps it was destroyed, along with Archimedes himself in the siege of 212 BC. Once the boat left the harbour, therefore, the fate of his letter was no longer in his hands. But this was no ordinary letter: it was his *Method*.

In the Library

The town of Aswan, in Egypt, lies on the Tropic of Cancer. This means that at noon on 21 June the walls of its buildings cast no shadows. Not so the walls of Alexandria. At the same date and time a small shadow will line their northern edges. Even though the walls of both towns are vertical, and even though the sun's rays are nearly parallel, the walls stand at different angles to those rays. It follows that the vertical walls of Aswan are at a seven-degree angle from the vertical walls of Alexandria. To Eratosthenes it was obvious that the surface of the Earth itself, the ground upon which the walls of both towns stood, was curved. By measuring the distance from Aswan to Alexandria, which accounts for 7 of the 360 degrees into which the circumference of the Earth can be divided, one could estimate that circumference. Eratosthenes thought this through in the third century BC, and came up with the value of 250,000 stadia, where 1 stadion is 125 paces, or about 625 feet. This is astonishingly close to the value accepted today (24,900 miles) – a smart calculation. For feats like this Archimedes addressed the *Method* to Eratosthenes. It may have been because Eratosthenes also knew a lot about a lot of subjects that he was appointed Director of the Library at Alexandria in 235 BC.

Alexandria was a young city in Eratosthenes' day. It was founded on 7 April 331 BC by Alexander the Great, and it soon replaced Memphis as the capital of Egypt. From 305 BC it was ruled by Ptolemy I Soter, of Greco-Macedonian ancestry, and the dynasty that he founded was to rule Egypt until Cleopatra's suicide in 30 BC. Under the Ptolemies, Alexandria became a great centre of Greek culture. By 280 BC a Temple to the Muses – the world's first museum – had been created. Built in the palace complex, it was a set of buildings, including a large dining hall, a covered walk and an arcade with recesses and seats, for the use of a scholarly community. It was here that Eratosthenes and other scholars spent their days, pacing the covered walk, speculating on such subjects as the circumference of the Earth, and occasionally receiving letters from their friend Archimedes. Their library constituted the greatest collection of texts in the ancient world. It had grown rapidly in the previous fifty years, as scholars had set out to record systematically the sum of world learning as it then existed. In the middle of the third century BC a catalogue of the library was attempted by Callimachus of Cyrene, entitled 'Catalogues of the authors eminent in various disciplines'. It was a monumental achievement. It took up 120 rolls. It was divided into categories, and within each category authors were discussed alphabetically, based upon the first letter of their name.

It would not have taken more than a couple of weeks for the ship bearing Archimedes' letter from Syracuse to arrive at the port of Alexandria, as it had a following wind. After having made a sacrifice to Poseidon for a safe voyage, someone would have taken the roll to its intended recipient – the safest of all hands, the learned and responsible lover of rolls Eratosthenes. Eratosthenes probably placed his letter from Archimedes in a section of the library devoted to science texts, and it rested there beside other rolls containing different treatises by the same author. It is more than likely that Eratosthenes had copies made of the letter; judging by Archimedes' hope that later generations would read the letter, this must certainly have been his expectation. One of the copies may have been stored in the precincts of the Temple of Serapis, nearby. The scrolls in the Serapeum, as it was called, were copied from those in the museum, and were available not just to the scholars leading their sequestered life, but also to members of the public. Eratosthenes lived to be about 80 years old. In his later years he was blind, and he is said to have committed suicide by voluntary starvation. But he had done all he could for Archimedes, and it was enough – just.

We know that Archimedes' letter to Eratosthenes arrived in Alexandria only because we know that it was read there. In the first century AD someone retrieved a copy of it. We even know the name of this person: he was called Hero. Hero wrote a treatise – *Metrica* – which mentions the *Method*: 'The same Archimedes shows in the same book [the *Method*] that if in a cube two cylinders penetrate whose bases are tangent to the faces of the cube, the common segment of the cylinders will be two thirds of the cube. This is useful for vaults constructed in this way . . .'

Hero seems to have been interested in Archimedes for the construction of a groin vault, in which cylindrical spaces are carved out of rectilinear masonry. This was a speciality of Hero's, and he also wrote a treatise on vaulting. We will see again and again, while tracing the survival of Archimedes' treatises, that they were of interest to those who wanted to apply his knowledge to real-world technical problems.

Note, though, how thin is the trail of evidence by which we can trace the history of Archimedes' works. Hero's *Metrica* itself survived only in one manuscript, and we can place him in Alexandria in the first century AD only because the Sun, the Moon, and the Earth have extremely regular movements in relation to one another: in another treatise – *Dioptra* – Hero gives an eyewitness account of an eclipse of the Moon, which he states took place on the tenth day before the vernal equinox beginning at Alexandria in the fifth watch of the night. Otto Neugebauer, the great figure of ancient mathematical astronomy, observed that this corresponds to an eclipse in AD 62 and to no other for centuries on either side of this date. And for centuries on either side of this date we hear nothing further of the *Method* itself.

A Change of Medium

Nothing is more dangerous for the contents of old documents than an information-technology upgrade, because mass data transfer has to take place, and somebody has to do it. The transition from the roll to the codex – the book format we know today – was a revolution in the history of data storage (see fig 3.1).

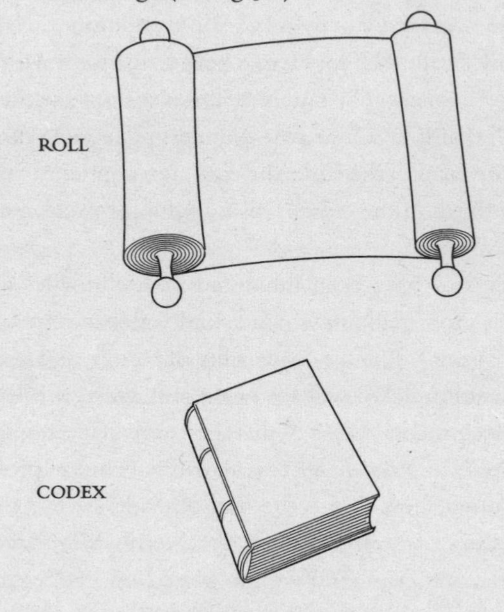

FIGURE 3.1

The introduction of codices was gradual; it started in the first century AD, but only by the end of the fourth century was it more or less complete. To me, the great surprise is that it took so long. The genius of the codex is that it contains knowledge not in two dimensions, like a roll, but three. The roll has height and width; the codex also has depth. Because it has depth, it doesn't need to be nearly as wide: a codex with 200 folios (400 pages), 6 inches wide, has the same potential data-storage area as a roll of the same height that is 200 feet long. And since each leaf of a codex is so thin, you save on an awful lot of width for a very small increase in depth. What's more, to access data on your roll you have to travel through the width dimension, while to access the data you need in a codex, you bypass the width and travel through the depth dimension, which is just a couple of inches thick. There's a big difference between 'unrolling' and 'thumbing through'. If you are consulting a catalogue listed alphabetically, getting to Archimedes is not a problem; but what about Zeno? With a codex you could just flip to the folios at the end and then close the codex, but you would have to unravel nearly the whole of your roll to get to your few lines about Zeno, and then reroll it. This did not happen, of course. If the catalogue were of any length, this literally could not have happened. This is why Callimachus' catalogue consisted of 120 rolls. If Callimachus' rolls were ever transcribed into codices, there would have been a lot less than 120 of them.

Ancient texts that didn't make the transition from roll to codex simply disappeared. The ancients shunned their rolls for the same reasons that we neglect our 78 rpm vinyl records: they had become an outmoded storage system. Only decades ago 78 rpm records were the preferred medium for music recordings, but now they are more often found in dustbins than on turntables. Similarly, the fragmentary remains of ancient texts can now be found in the dustbins of the ancient world. If Archimedes' letter to Eratosthenes had stayed in its roll, it would have been at first neglected, then abandoned and finally it would have crumbled to dust. In fact, the copy (or copies) that stayed in rolls did just that, though no fragments of Archimedes have been found in dustbins.

And just because Archimedes was famous, it doesn't mean that his works were an obvious priority in the IT upgrade. In truth, even though he was legendary, Archimedes was hardly ever read. The most important of his results, like his approximation for the value of pi, became well known and well used, but few people actually read his arguments; they were simply too difficult. And here Archimedes was at a particular disadvantage compared to other great thinkers in antiquity. The Homers, the Platos and the Euclids of this world were recognised at the time as not only great but also fundamental, and therefore they were frequently used and, in due course, copied into codices. Archimedes was too difficult to be fundamental; very few people could understand him. His genius actually worked against him. His texts were very often left unrolled, and they were always going to have had a tough time getting into codices. Three hundred years after Hero another mathematician called Pappus discussed a treatise by Archimedes on semi-regular polyhedra. Of this treatise no trace remains. Perhaps it never made it into a codex. It lost the race against destruction right there.

The person who did more than anyone else to ensure the survival of Archimedes' treatises through this decisive period was named Eutocius. Eutocius was born in Ascalon in Palestine, in about AD 480. He didn't just read Archimedes's treatises: he researched them and explained them. Eutocius travelled widely among the great centres of learning at the time, including to Alexandria, where he must have met a teacher called Ammonius. Eutocius dedicated his first work on Archimedes, a commentary on *Sphere and Cylinder I*, to Ammonius, and clearly held him in high regard. In his preface Eutocius says that he would write commentaries on other treatises by Archimedes if Ammonius approved of this one. Ammonius must have done so, because Eutocius went on to write three further commentaries – on *Sphere and Cylinder II*, on the *Measurement of the Circle* and on *Balancing Planes*. Eutocius had to struggle to find Archimedes' writings. Whether they were in codices already, or still in rolls, there weren't very many of them. At one point in *Sphere and Cylinder II* Archimedes promises to prove a mathematical point but never does. Eutocius therefore went on a search. He writes: 'In a certain old manuscript (for we did not cease from the search of many manuscripts) we have read theorems written very unclearly (because of the errors), and in many ways mistaken about the diagrams. But they had to do with the subject matter we were looking for, and they preserved in part the Doric dialect Archimedes liked using, written with the ancient name of things.' Eutocius then included an account of this text in his commentary.

Eutocius' treatises survive together with the works of Archimedes that they comment upon. And this is an important point. Eutocius, like everybody else, clearly saw the advantages of the new IT, and exploited it. Just as a CD can store a great many more Bach cantatas than a 78, so a single codex can contain many more of Archimedes' treatises than a roll. Eutocius, it seems, prepared an edition of several of Archimedes' treatises, together with his commentaries, and had them bound within wooden boards. From the sixth century onwards we should imagine a treatise by Archimedes inside a handy parchment codex, placed safely within wooden covers and nestled comfortably with other letters of a similar nature.

The Gathering Storm

Archimedes' letter to Eratosthenes might have been comfortable, but it was by no means safe. Times were changing, and they were not changing to Archimedes' advantage. One by one the great cities of the ancient world, which held the ancient schools of learning and the books upon which they depended, were pillaged by invaders. Rome was sacked by the Goths in 410, Antioch by the Persians in 540, and Athens by the Slavs in 580. There may have been many copies of Archimedes' letters outside Alexandria in the third century AD; there were hardly any by the end of the sixth. Things were little better in Alexandria itself. In about AD 270 the Emperor Aurelian, in his war against Zenobia, damaged a large part of the palace complex that contained the museum. In 391 Theophilus, the Archbishop of Alexandria, sacked the Serapeum, the daughter library of the museum. In 415 the distinguished female mathematician Hypatia was torn to pieces by a fanatic and ignorant Christian mob. Archimedes' letters had to get out of Alexandria before they suffered a similar fate.

As the ancient world disappeared, its gods went with it. And as Christianity became the official religion of the Roman Empire, many classical texts, if they were not condemned as dangerous, were dismissed as irrelevant. It is not that Christians wilfully destroyed them very often; they just ceased to copy them. Scribes put their energies into Christian texts. The Christian curriculum necessarily included some ancient authors – Homer was necessary for Rhetoric, and Euclid for Geometry; but Archimedes was not included in the curriculum of Salvation. Fewer people than ever before had the resources to read him, and even fewer would have read him even if they could.

In the fifth and sixth centuries, for every donkey that Archimedes could ride on, there were hordes of thoroughbred barbarians. The race against destruction for all classical texts was getting increasingly desperate. The only question was where could they run to? The only answer was Constantinople.

Into the Ark

John Dean and I flew to Constantinople, present-day Istanbul, in search of Archimedes. The city was founded on the Bosphorus by Constantine, the first Christian Emperor, on Monday, 11 May AD 330. He founded it specifically as the capital of the eastern Roman Empire. Constantinople was a relative newcomer to the Mediterranean world of learning. Successive emperors poured the resources that only they could marshal into making the city worthy of the empire that it inherited. Certainly the emphasis was on Christian works: indeed Constantine ordered fifty complete copies of the Bible to be written at this time. But the classics were also a concern in Constantinople. In an address to the Emperor Constantius on Wednesday, 1 January 357, the philosopher Themistius described a plan to guarantee the survival of ancient literature. He proposed a scriptorium – a writing centre – for the production of new copies of the classics, which would ensure that the new capital of the empire became a centre of culture. The plan may have been put into effect: in 372 an order was issued to the city prefect Clearchus to appoint four scribes skilled in Greek, and three in Latin, to undertake the transcription and repair of books. In 425 the Emperor Theodosius II established an imperial foundation for literary and philosophical studies. Even more importantly, in 412 he built massive walls around the city.

John Dean and I didn't have to look far to find Archimedes: his geometry is indelibly stamped on Constantinople. Between 532 and 537 the Emperor Justinian crowned the 'New Rome' with one of the greatest buildings the world has ever seen – the Church of Hagia Sophia. This is how a contemporary, Procopius describes it:

> A construction of masonry rises from the ground, not in a straight line, but gradually drawing back from its sides and receding in the middle, so as to describe a semi-circular shape which is called a half-cylinder by specialists, and this towers to a precipitous height. The extremity of this structure terminates in the fourth part of a sphere, and above it another crescent-shaped form is lifted up by the adjoining parts of the building . . . On either side of these, columns are placed on the ground, and these, too, do not stand in a straight line, but retreat inward in a half-circle as if making way for one another in a dance, and above them is suspended a crescent-shaped form.

Hagia Sophia is an astonishing building on many levels, but the important point here is that it was designed with diagrams and by numbers. It was necessarily the work of mathematicians. One of them was Anthemius of Tralles – Anthemius who wrote texts on *Burning Mirrors* and on *Remarkable Mechanical Devices*. The second architect was somewhat younger than Anthemius. His name was Isidore of Miletus, and he wrote a commentary on Hero of Alexandria's own treatise on *Vaulting*. Anthemius and Isidore were masters of Archimedes' discipline, and the plan of Hagia Sophia might well resemble the figure that was inscribed on Archimedes' tomb.

The mathematical world was small in the sixth century, and it was getting smaller all the time. It is not surprising that Anthemius and Isidore were well acquainted with Eutocius. Eutocius dedicated his commentaries on the works of Apollonius of Perga to Anthemius. And Isidore knew Eutocius' works on Archimedes extremely well.

The text of Eutocius' commentary on *Sphere and Cylinder I* is preserved because it was copied by one of Isidore's students. When he had finished his copying, this student wrote: 'The commentary of Eutocius of Ascalon on the first book of Archimedes "On the Sphere and the Cylinder", the edition being collated by the Milesian mechanical author, Isidore, our teacher'. Isidore, then, was preparing an edition of Archimedes' works, together with Eutocius' commentaries, in Constantinople.

Archimedes made it to Constantinople in the nick of time. For three hundred years after the time of Isidore, his writings, like most of the classics, disappear from recorded history. The empire that centred on the city became embroiled in internal strife (about holy images), and was subject to external threats (from barbarians and Arabs). When texts were read at all, they were read to bolster particularly contentious aspects of Christian doctrine. Constantinople itself did the one thing it had to do for Archimedes, and for so many ancient authors: it survived. It was the only city of the ancient world of any consequence to survive unmolested into the Middle Ages. Constantinople served as the ark for ancient literature, and the Noah of the classics was the Emperor Theodosius. A hundred years before Isidore built his great church, Theodosius had already constructed the city's massive walls to weather the Dark Age storm.

The Byzantine Renaissance

On Saturday, 26 July 811, Krum, the Bulgarian Khan, slew Nicephorus, the Byzantine Emperor, at the battle of Pliska and turned his skull into a wine cup. Not a good start to the ninth century for Constantinople. On the surface things didn't look much better thirty years and six emperors later, when Michael III, 'The Drunkard', ascended the throne. But in fact the intellectual climate was improving, and it got even better when Basil I assassinated Michael in 867. Under Basil I Constantinople quickly became the capital of the greatest empire in the Mediterranean world. The Macedonian dynasty that he founded could boast both scholarship and mettle. While Constantine VII wrote a book on the administration of the empire, Basil II took 14,000 Bulgarians prisoner in 1014, and blinded ninety-nine out of every hundred. The lucky one in a hundred got to guide his fellows home. Constantinople had entered a golden age, if not an enlightened one.

The famous Byzantine 'rebirth' of the ninth and tenth centuries produced impressive buildings and consummate works of art. John and I could still see and film the Imperial Palace, and when we got back to Baltimore we could photograph Henry Walters' own fabulously illuminated Byzantine manuscripts. But the most important thing about this cultural revival is that as scholars started reading the classics that had been lying neglected in their libraries, so they started copying them. The most voracious reader of them all was a distinguished civil servant, and twice Patriarch of Constantinople, by the name of Photius. His *Bibliotheca* is a compilation of works that he had read, with a summary of the contents, style and biography of the author. As Nigel Wilson puts it, with the *Bibliotheca* Photius had invented the book review. The *Bibliotheca* is invaluable for many reasons, but prominent among them is that it gives us a good idea of the extraordinary variety of classical texts that were still extant in Constantinople in Photius' day. Admittedly, scholars thought that some of Photius' claims were a bit rich. He claimed, for example, to have read works by Hyperides, an ancient Greek orator. Since no one else in Constantinople even mentioned whole texts by Hyperides, and since none now survives in codex form, this, it was thought, was unlikely. Nonetheless, the statistics gleaned from Photius are impressive. For example, of the thirty-three historians that he discusses the works of twenty are now unknown.

When ninth-century scribes copied classical texts they wrote in a fundamentally different script from that used in Isidore's day. Before the ninth century texts were written in capital letters, technically called majuscules. After the ninth century, generally speaking, they

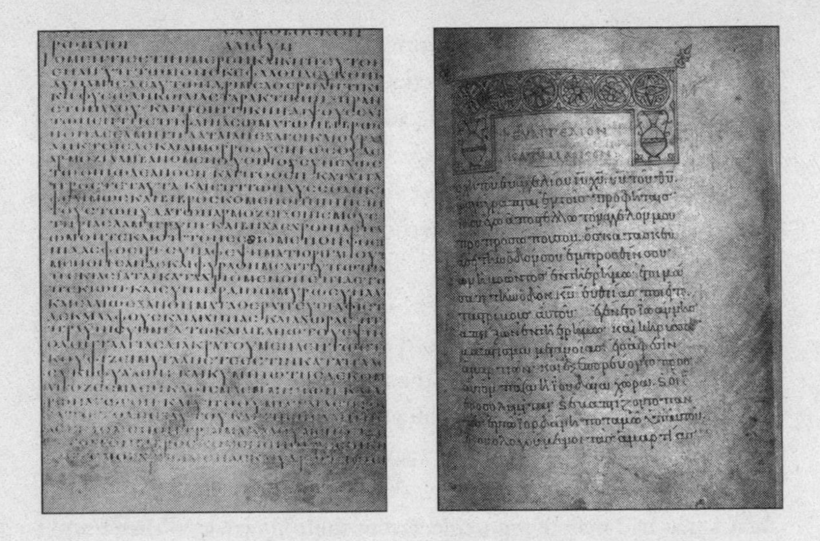

FIGURE 3.2 *Majuscules (left) and Miniscules (right)*

were written in a new script, technically called minuscule, whose letters – unlike capitals – could be written joined up and were designed to take up less space (see fig 3.2).

The origins of minuscule script are probably in the letters, documents and accounts of the civil service based in Constantinople. Minuscule script was faster to write, its letters were easier to form, and with it one could fit many more words on a folio than was possible with capitals. By the middle of the ninth century it was also used for religious and scientific texts. Many codices, written in capitals in the sixth century and before, were systematically transcribed into lower-case script. This change in how texts were copied was quite as important a hurdle for Archimedes' texts to jump as the transition from roll to codex, and for a similar reason. So few majuscule codices from the fifth and sixth centuries survive that ninth-century scholars may have destroyed their majuscule manuscripts after they had made minuscule copies. The majuscule codices may have been increasingly difficult to read, and after they had been transcribed there was no need for them. The texts of nearly all ancient Greek authors are each dependent on just a very few minuscule manuscripts copied in Constantinople in the ninth and tenth centuries. Archimedes is no exception. He was actually dependent on three manuscripts.

And this is the fundamental point. All that stuff that Reviel has talked about, and will go on to talk about, survives because of just three physical objects, of which the codex on my desk is one.

The ABC of Archimedes

These three objects are called Codex A, Codex B and Codex C. They had some texts in common: all three contained *Balancing Planes*; A and B contained *Quadrature of the Parabola*; A and C contained *Sphere and Cylinder*, *Measurement of the Circle*, and *Spiral Lines*; and B and C contained *On Floating Bodies*. Codex A was the unique witness to *Conoids and Spheroids* and *Sand-Reckoner*; Codex C is the unique witness to *Method* and *Stomachion*.

It seems very likely that all three codices are the fruit of a revival of interest in Archimedes' texts early in the ninth century. When a scribe finished copying Archimedes' *Quadrature of the Parabola* in Codex A, he wrote a little note of adulation, but not to Archimedes. He wrote: 'Leo the geometer, may you flourish – May you live many a year, dear friend of the Muses.' This Leo was almost certainly the Leo who was giving private instruction in Constantinople in the 820s. Known as Leo the Philosopher, he was evidently a talented teacher; one student who had read Euclid under his supervision was captured by the Arabs in 830. His report of Leo's learning was sufficient to cause the Caliph to invite Leo to Baghdad. Thankfully, he did not go. Leo was clearly something of a polymath, and a practical one at that. He built fire signal stations between Constantinople and the border of the empire. Should there be an emergency on the border north of Tarsus, a message could reach the capital in less than an hour. In the late 850s Leo's skills were rewarded, and he was appointed director of a school in the Imperial Palace. He must have played a prominent role in choosing the other professors. One of them was Theodore, a geometer. We are safe to assume that Archimedes was being studied and copied in the school of the Imperial Palace, and that the texts in Codex A were copied in that school. The accession of Basil I in 867 ensured that Archimedes' treatises could be studied in safety, at least for the time being.

We will trace the histories of the three manuscripts that contained Archimedes' treatises in more detail later. But for now it is important to know that Codices A and B survive no longer. We have only copies and translations of them. As a result, Codex C is not only the unique source for the *Method* and *Stomachion* and for *Floating Bodies* in Greek, it is also the oldest surviving manuscript of Archimedes' treatises in Greek, by over four hundred years. Codex C is on my desk, and now it is time to see how it was made.

Codex C

Codex C, like most medieval manuscripts, is not written on paper; it is written on the backs of animals. The skin of an animal is such a refined product of natural selection that it is hard to see how it could be used for much else. But skin has two great qualities: it is supple, enabling movement, and it is tough, allowing animals to sustain all manner of knocks. Skin is well suited to life on earth outside of fire and too much water, and, with some treatment, the same properties do in fact make it an excellent, durable writing surface. With that treatment, it is called parchment.

Parchment was invented at Pergamum in Asia Minor – or so legend has it. King Eumenes II wanted his library to match that of Alexandria, so the Ptolemies put an embargo on the export of papyrus from Egypt at the beginning of the second century BC. Parchment was Eumenes' home-grown substitute. Be that as it may, it was with the introduction of the codex that parchment came into its own. While papyrus certainly has tensile strength, it fractures more easily than parchment if you fold it. Since they consisted of folded sheets, codices made of parchment survived better than those made of papyrus. Parchment is more durable than paper, which is why certificates and awards meant to last are sometimes still inscribed on sheepskins.

Making parchment is not everybody's idea of fun. Certainly not Reviel's – he's a vegetarian. This is what you do. Kill the animals and drain the blood from their veins. Flay them; slit their underbellies, cut off their extremities and peel back the skin. Place the skins in a vat containing a weak solution of lime, which you can make by heating limestone. The lime solution is destructive to organic tissue: it breaks down the epidermis and the subcutaneous fat, and it weakens the bonds that attach the hair to the skin. The inner layer of the dermis alone remains intact. This layer is mainly made up of collagen. Collagen is a protein made up of three chains of amino acids that spiral around an elongated straight axis. The chains are staggered, and the resulting fibres have no definite terminal limits. Collagen is the crucial constituent of parchment; it is what makes it tough. After several days remove the skins from the vat, place them over a beam and scrape them down with a dull blade. Once you have removed the worst of the fat and the hair, attach the skins to wooden frames. As they dry they will contract and become taut. Once they are taut, scrape them again, this time with a very sharp half-moon-shaped blade. Cut them from their frames and you will have your parchment.

Imagine a set of newspapers stacked in a pile, sandwiched between wooden boards, and the whole lot stitched together, and you actually have a good first approximation of the physical construction of a tenth-century Byzantine manuscript. The newspapers, called quires, usually consisted of four nested double sheets, called bifolios (see fig. 3.3). This makes up eight sheets of a newspaper (sixteen pages), but remember that manuscript people call them folios. Since you could get two bifolios out of each sheep, twenty-four sheep would have been needed to make enough bifolios for the surviving parchment in the Archimedes manuscript. To make the quires you had to cut the skins to size, rub them with a pumice stone to raise a nap and give them a transparent glaze mainly consisting of egg white. This was the support that housed the texts of Archimedes and the others.

FIGURE 3.3
A Quire

And now to the ink. This is more fun to make. You start with a solution of gallic acid. Gallic acid is present in oak galls, which are growths on oak trees – the tree's response to infection from insects and mites. It is made up of carbon, hydrogen and oxygen, and it has the power to contract organic tissues such as collagen. This will allow the ink to etch into the parchment and therefore remain in place. Crush the galls and boil them in water. To this solution add ferrous sulphate, sometimes called green vitriol or copperas. This will supply most of the colour to the ink. It is a compound of iron and sulphuric acid that you can frequently find together with pyrite. You then need to add a thickening agent to this solution. By a process called gummosis, some trees belonging to the family Fabaceae produce gum from their bark if under attack. Gum Arabic is produced by the acacia tree, which grows in Africa. Gum tragacanth, produced by several shrubs of the genus *Astragalus*, principally astragalus gummier, can be found in Asia Minor. If you are making a manuscript in Constantinople, you might find it easier to get hold of gum tragacanth. It is still used today to coat pills. To produce it in the quantity sufficient to satisfy the pharmaceutical industry, incisions are made into the bark and wooden wedges are driven into the incisions. The chemical make-up of gum is complicated and varied, but it contains carbon, hydrogen, oxygen and metals such as calcium, magnesium and potassium. Since the resulting mixture darkens only slowly as it oxidises on the parchment, you might want to add carbon black to it. This way you will be able to see what you are writing as you are writing it. Give the whole lot a good shake, and you have the ink that the scribes of manuscripts used to write their texts.

And so, about a hundred years after the death of Leo, a scribe prepared himself for a job. We can picture this scribe, because pictures of scribes writing actually survive from this period. When we catch sight of him, he has already been through familiar procedures. Guided by a ruler, he has made lines on the parchment to help him keep his columns of text straight, he has sharpened his reed pens on a stone and cut the nib down the middle to help the ink flow; he has prepared his ink and placed the inkwell on his table, and he has beside him a knife so that he can refine his pen or scrub out a mistake should he make one. He has prepared the tools of his trade, the mystic implements of the human voice. We see him seated in his chair, ready to write. He doesn't have a writing table, but then he doesn't need one. He is going to write on his lap, resting the parchment on a board. In front of him, on a stand, is a codex. This is the codex that he is going to copy.

But before we look at what he wrote, let's think a bit about the codex on that stand in front of him. Did this codex look like the codex that the scribe was about to make? Was it a sixth-century codex, from the time of Isidore, or was it written in minuscule? Was it one codex containing the same treatises in the same order, or should we actually be thinking about several codices, sequentially placed upon the stand? As yet, we do not know enough about the parent manuscript (or manuscripts) that our scribe used. Judging by the text, he did not copy any of his treatises from Codex A. It is certainly possible that he was copying a sixth-century manuscript, but the evidence is not conclusive. This is perhaps the most important unanswered question about our manuscript.

Be that as it may, the scribe did his job and wrote his text. Each folio that he wrote measured about 30 centimetres by 19.5. He wrote his text in two columns and wrote thirty-five lines in each column. He made a codex with generous margins, so together the columns were 24 centimetres high and 14.5 wide. Of course, Archimedes' letter to Eratosthenes – the *Method* – was just one of the texts he copied. The manuscript currently starts towards the end of *Balancing Planes*, followed by *Floating Bodies*, and only then comes the *Method*. The *Method* is followed by *Spiral Lines*, *Sphere and Cylinder*, *Measurement of the Circle* and finally by one folio of *Stomachion*. Our scribe was an expert, writing in a minuscule script characteristic of the third quarter of the tenth century. Nigel Wilson says that his handwriting is somewhat similar to that in a manuscript, with the date 988, now in the Monastery of St John the Theologian, on the island of Patmos. The scribe didn't understand what he was copying but, as Reviel will explain later, this was a good thing. We can assume that he worked for no longer than a few months. We can only guess at the true extent of the original codex, though, because we are now missing the beginning, the end and several chunks in the middle. In fact, it is perfectly possible that originally the manuscript contained yet more of Archimedes' treatises.

The codex our scribe wrote was actually a typical product of the Byzantine Renaissance of the ninth and tenth centuries. As with most Byzantine manuscripts, we do not know who commissioned it, or even who read it. In fact, judging by the lack of marginal comments in it, it does not seem to have been used very much. But none of this matters: it is the unique source for the *Method*, *Stomachion*, and *On Floating Bodies* in Greek. If our scribe did nothing else in his long life, his was a life well spent.

This is a story of survival, achieved against all the odds, through an extravagant process by which creation just managed to outrun destruction. Many rolls have crumbled; many codices have burned. I have brought you to the earliest surviving text of Archimedes – the thoughts of Archimedes preserved in a very highly ordered arrangement of flesh and iron. But it was made in the tenth century – closer to our own time than to the time of Archimedes. Tenth-century parchment codices look nothing like third-century BC rolls. As Archimedes' letters were copied, so they were transformed, and the treatises that survive no longer look anything like the letters that Archimedes himself wrote. Archimedes would not have recognised them, could not have read them. This is important, but to explain why, we need again to consult the expert.

4
Visual Science

There's a lot one can learn from manuscripts. For one thing, we can pick up what's written in them. We can find out what thoughts Archimedes had, in Syracuse, in the third century BC. We can find out how such thoughts came to influence all of later science.

And we can do more: we can use manuscripts to find out not just what thoughts past scholars had but also how they came to think such thoughts. How did Archimedes think through his mathematics? How did his readers? Such questions are raised by a recent, cognitive turn in science studies. To answer such questions we must turn to manuscripts, for they provide us with the unique source of evidence for this fundamental question: how does science register in the mind's eye?

In fact, we all have, nowadays, a rather clear image of science, in our mind's eye. Just as an illustration of that, let us consider the following experiment. In fig. 4.1 I show two pictures of open pages from books. Take a look for a minute: even though the illustrations are too small to be read comfortably, they allow us immediately to make certain judgements. We just *know* that the left-hand page is scientific. It is, in fact, from an introductory text in the calculus (the subject pioneered by Archimedes, to which we shall return). The right-hand page is from James Joyce's *Finnegans Wake* (and is, incidentally, much more difficult to read than the left-hand page.)

When publishers say they are afraid of publishing popular science that 'looks technical', what they mean is that they want their pages to look like the right-hand, not the left-hand page. What are readers

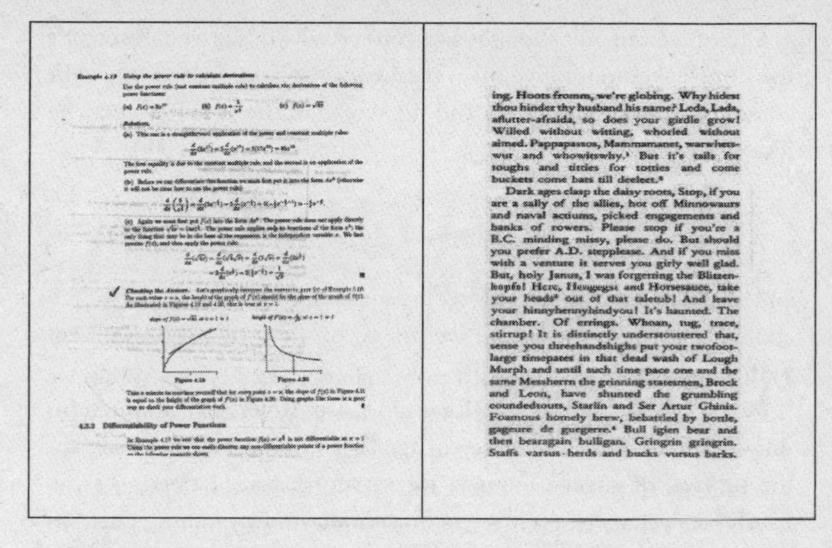

ing. Hoots fromm, we're globing. Why hidest thou hinder thy husband his name? Leda, Lada, aflutter-afraida, so does your girdle grow! Willed without witting, whorled without aimed. Pappapassos, Mammamanet, warwhetswut and whowitswhy.[1] But it's tails for toughs and titties for totties and come buckets come bats till deeleet.[2]

Dark ages clasp the daisy roots, Stop, if you are a sally of the allies, hot off Minnowaurs and naval actiums, picked engagements and banks of rowers. Please stop if you're a B.C. minding missy, please do. But should you prefer A.D. stepplease. And if you miss with a venture it serves you girly well glad. But, holy Janus, I was forgetting the Blitzenhopfs! Here, Hengegst and Horsesauce, take your heads[3] out of that taletub! And leave your hinnyhennyhindyou! It's haunted. The chamber. Of errings. Whoan, tug, trace, stirrup! It is distinctly understouttered that, sense you threehandshighs put your twofootlarge timepates in that dead wash of Lough Murph and until such time pace one and the same Messherrn the grinning statesmen, Brock and Leon, have shunted the grumbling coundedtouts, Starlin and Ser Artur Ghinis. Foamous homely brew, bebattled by bottle, gageure de guegerre.[4] Bull igien bear and then bearagain bulligan. Gringrin gringrin. Staffs versus herds and bucks versus barks.

FIGURE 4.1

today afraid of? They are afraid of *equations*. With good reason: they were force-fed such equations for several, terrible years of their childhood and adolescence. The result is that we tend, first, to hate equations and, second, to consider them to be the natural format of science as such. Both assumptions are wrong. Equations are a great invention – they should be respected, if not loved – and they are not natural. Instead, they are a historical invention whose origins lie in such documents as the Palimpsest. The Greeks did not use equations. Archimedes did not use equations. Their science looked nothing like the left-hand page in the figure.

Before Equations

Equations make logic visible. Suppose you say: 'The first together with the second is equal to the third; therefore the first is equal to the third minus the second.'

Give it a moment's thought and you see why this is true. But that's the trouble: you must give this a moment's thought; meanwhile your attention has wandered away and the thread of the argument may be lost. Write instead:

$$A + B = C, \text{ therefore}$$
$$A = C - B$$

and it works effortlessly: we *see* how the argument runs. Now no attention is thrown away and we can go on following the argument with great ease.

We see how the same information acts differently through its different interfaces. The different media are important not only for the survival of science but also for its very nature. Indeed, we can hardly understand Greek science without understanding, first, its essential interface. This, however, was not the equation. It was the diagram.

Greek Mathematics was a Visual Science

The starting point, as ever, should be at Syracuse. In particular, begin with the story already recounted above from Cicero: the tomb of Archimedes. We recall Cicero finding, after much effort, a desolate, neglected slab of stone and on it the message that Archimedes chose as his symbol: a diagram showing a sphere and a cylinder. This was the self-chosen symbol of science. Once again we make the inevitable comparison to Einstein. What was Einstein's symbol, the emblem that immediately comes to mind? No, I don't mean the protruding tongue; I mean this:

$$E = mc^2$$

You have seen this emblem endless times. It has become a kind of symbol not only of Einstein but of science in general. And it is, of course, an equation. So here is the starting point, in a nutshell: modern science is a science of equations; ancient science was a science of diagrams.

In the ancient exact sciences – not only mathematics but also astronomy and mechanics – and in many other fields, such as musical theory, diagrams would always occupy centre stage. The text is made of individual 'propositions', each making a point, proving that so-and-so is the case. The late British historian of Greek mathematics David Fowler used to say that each proposition is 'drawing a figure and then telling a story about it'. Everything is about those figures, done for the sake of those figures.

Diagrams, of course, are also used in modern science; but there is a big difference. In modern science diagrams serve as a kind of illustration; they are there to make the experience of learning science somewhat less traumatic for the student, but they are not part of the logic of the argument itself. In modern science it is considered crucial to make sure that no information depends on the diagram, otherwise one could end up with a false argument such as is demonstrated in figure 4.2.

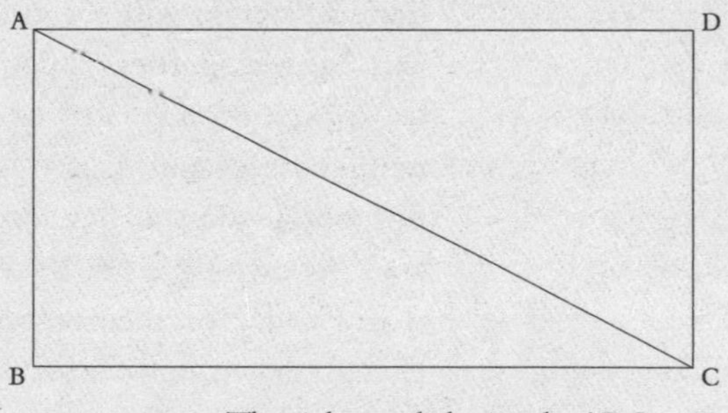

FIGURE 4.2 *The right-angled triangle ABC*

The area of a triangle is the product of its two sides, divided by two.

Proof: we draw a triangle ABC. The two smaller sides are AB, BC. On the longer side AC we apply another triangle, exactly identical to the triangle ABC, namely the triangle ACD. The result is a rectangle ABCD. The area of this rectangle is obviously the product of the two sides AB, BC. The triangle ABC is obviously exactly half the rectangle ABCD (after all, the two triangles ABC, ACD are identical). So that the area of a triangle is the product of its two sides divided by two, QED.

What is wrong about this proof? Well, it assumes something just on the basis of the diagram, even though there is no basis in the text for making such an assumption. In the diagram we happened to draw a right-angled triangle. In a right-angled triangle the claim of the proof follows. But it does not follow in other triangles (see fig. 4.3, where the product of the two sides AB and BC is clearly more than double the area of the triangle!). In short, we thought we were talking about triangles in general, but inadvertently we slipped into talking about right-angled triangles, all because we have taken the diagram on faith. And so modern philosophers and logicians are adamant: do not rely on the diagram!

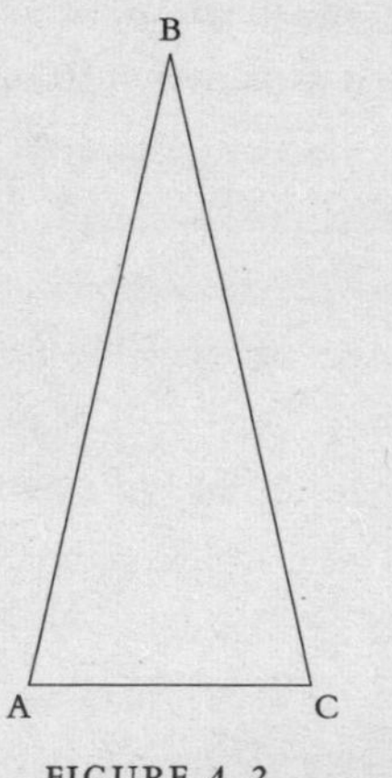

FIGURE 4.3

The logical and philosophical issue is deep: language is general, but a diagram is a particular thing. You see, you cannot draw a diagram without its having some particular properties. Suppose I wanted to draw a triangle so that its angle is neither right-angled, nor acute-angled, nor obtuse-angled, but just a 'general' angle – how would I do that? I cannot do that. I've got on the page some definite triangle drawn, and because it is a definite triangle, it also has some definite angle. Language, on the other hand, is more forgiving. I can say, 'Let there be a triangle,' and because I did not say *which* triangle – I just said '*a* triangle' – I am allowed to think of it as right-angled, obtuse-angled or acute-angled. And so the modern philosophers and the logicians insist: to make sure the logic of the proof works in its full, most general form, we must rely on the language alone and never on the diagram.

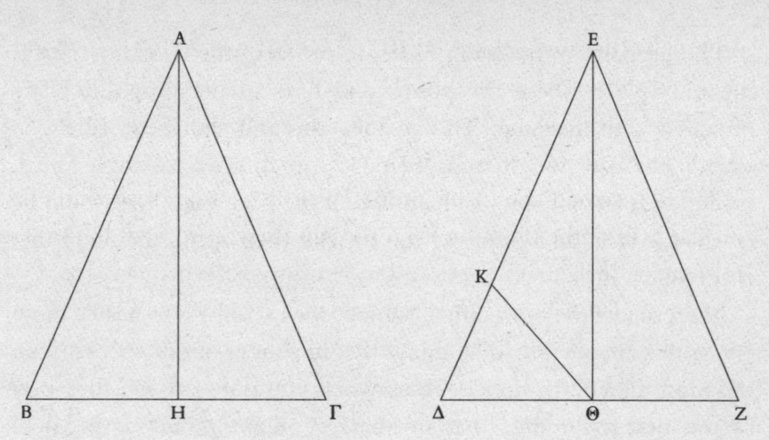

FIGURE 4.4 *Two isosceles cones*

Which is precisely what Greek mathematicians did and, incredibly, without making any logical errors. This is one of the great puzzles about Greek mathematics: it is thoroughly diagrammatic – and also thoroughly precise. The Greek mathematicians never made mistakes such as the trivial one mentioned above, not even in subtle and indirect ways. Greek mathematics is as precise as modern mathematics. How come? In a few pages, I shall try to provide an answer.

Let us first of all see how Greek mathematicians did in fact rely on the diagram. The following is from the first book on *Sphere and Cylinder* – the work eternalised on Archimedes' tomb. As mentioned already, Archimedes had a sly manner of writing – clever and playful, always hiding the main point of attack from the reader until the last moment. It should therefore come as no surprise that, until late in the book, spheres and cylinders are hardly mentioned. Instead, Archimedes keeps referring to *cones*. Here, for example, is proposition 17 (see fig. 4.4):

Let there be two isosceles cones ΑΒΓ, ΔΕΖ, and let the base of the cone ΑΒΓ be equal to the surface of the cone ΔΕΖ, and let the height ΑΗ be equal to the perpendicular ΚΘ drawn from the centre of the base Θ, on one side of the cone (such as ΔΕ); I say that the cones are equal.

The proposition makes its claim in terms of the diagram. This is the only place where the points and lines of the proposition are provided with meaning. This is done through alphabetic labels, in exactly the way we do today; in fact, in this we follow a Greek invention. (The Chinese had a different method: each line would be labelled as if it had a different colour. But then again, their alphabet is very different.)

Now, one of the most difficult things for a scholar is to notice those things that are obvious. The things that lie 'under our noses' are often the most difficult to notice – but, when you notice them, they may be the most rewarding. I had one such moment in considering such simple passages as these in Greek mathematics. I made this observation in the first chapter of my PhD thesis and, quite frankly, it is the one thing most of my peers know about my work. I shall probably die, and still be mentioned as 'the guy who made that observation on Greek diagrams' – which I find quite annoying, seeing that this was about the first thing I ever did as a scholar. (I do like to think it was not all downhill from there!) Still, it is an important observation – because it definitely shows that Greek mathematicians did not work the way modern philosophers and logicians wish that they had. They most certainly relied on the diagram.

Because, you see: in an expression such as 'the cones ΑΒΓ, ΔΕΖ' we may easily guess that the points ΑΒΓ, ΔΕΖ each stand for the vertices of a triangle cutting through the cone (see fig. 4.4). But how are we to know the individual distribution of the letters? In each cone, two letters must stand on the base, and one on the top – but which is which? This is what makes this observation so difficult to make: because visual information is so powerful, the moment we are in front of a diagram we immediately 'read off' the information and establish that ΒΓ, ΔΖ are bases, Α, Ε are tops; and we even fail to notice that *the text said no such thing*. In fact, this is the general rule throughout Greek mathematics: the identity of objects is not established by the words but by the diagrams. The diagrams are there not as some kind of illustration, so as to make the reading experience more pleasant; the diagrams are there to provide us with the most basic information. They tell us the who's who of the proposition: which letter stands next to which object. Ancient diagrams are not illustrative, they are informative; they constitute part of the logic of the proposition. And so, Greek science was a visual science.

How come, then, that Greek mathematicians did not make trivial mistakes based on the information in the diagram? How did they keep their perfect logic? The reason has to do with a very special interface used in Greek mathematics: the subtle, clever way in which diagrams are used.

The Sands of Syracuse

What did Archimedes' diagrams look like? As we can see now, following Will's explanation of the history of manuscripts, this is a question for which we have only very indirect evidence. The earliest evidence we have, in fact, is in the Palimpsest itself. One's first reaction might be that of despair: if our evidence is so far from the original, what chance do we have of ever getting there? How can we realistically hope to know what ancient diagrams looked like? Indeed, this is a difficult question. In principle, nothing guarantees that we can answer it. It could be that medieval scribes simply invented their own diagrams, instead of faithfully copying their ancient sources. After all, the modern editors very clearly do just that: they invent their own diagrams. When I set out on my study of the medieval diagrams of Archimedes, I couldn't tell whether the medieval scribes did the same or not. My greatest fear was that I should get to Paris, Rome, Venice and Florence, each time opening an old book and finding there a completely different diagram. If this had been the case, my conclusion would have had to be that the ancient diagrams just could not be reconstructed.

Instead, page after page, diagram after diagram, I opened those pages and they all showed effectively the same figure. Errors crept in, here but not there. Corrections were made in some manuscripts, not others (suggesting the original might have contained an error detected by some scribes). But it was clear that the diagrams were related. They were copied, not invented. In short, one could apply *the philological method*. We take separate manuscripts and compare them. If two separate manuscripts possess the same text – or diagram – this means that there must have been a common source to both. This then allows us to go back and infer an earlier form. And while we can never be sure that this earlier form goes all the way back to Archimedes, it is still very important to try to push our evidence back as far as possible.

This, then, must be stressed. Sometimes readers are disappointed to hear that not all of the works by Archimedes are represented by the Palimpsest alone. Some of the works are represented on the Palimpsest and also in the various descendants of Codex A. But this is not some kind of blemish on the value of the Palimpsest. To the contrary: for the philological method, it is of the utmost importance to have *more than one* source. Taken alone, the Palimpsest can tell us about the year AD 975. But whenever we can take the Palimpsest and compare it with other independent medieval sources, it can suddenly tell us much more. Whenever we find that both the Palimpsest and another independent medieval manuscript tell the same story – whenever this happens – we can push back the dates, probably to a source from Eutocius' time or before, following which the two traditions diverged. And this already makes us much closer to the world of Archimedes himself.

This work is of a complex character. After all, Codex A itself is no longer extant, so we have to apply the philological method twice over. My original project of studying the Archimedes manuscripts involved the descendants of Codex A alone (the Palimpsest, remember, was not available when I started on this work). So I looked at those manuscripts.

There are some 250 figures in the works of Archimedes, but let us take one example: in fig. 4.5 we can see the various variants of the diagram for *Sphere and Cylinder I*, proposition 38. On the basis of these

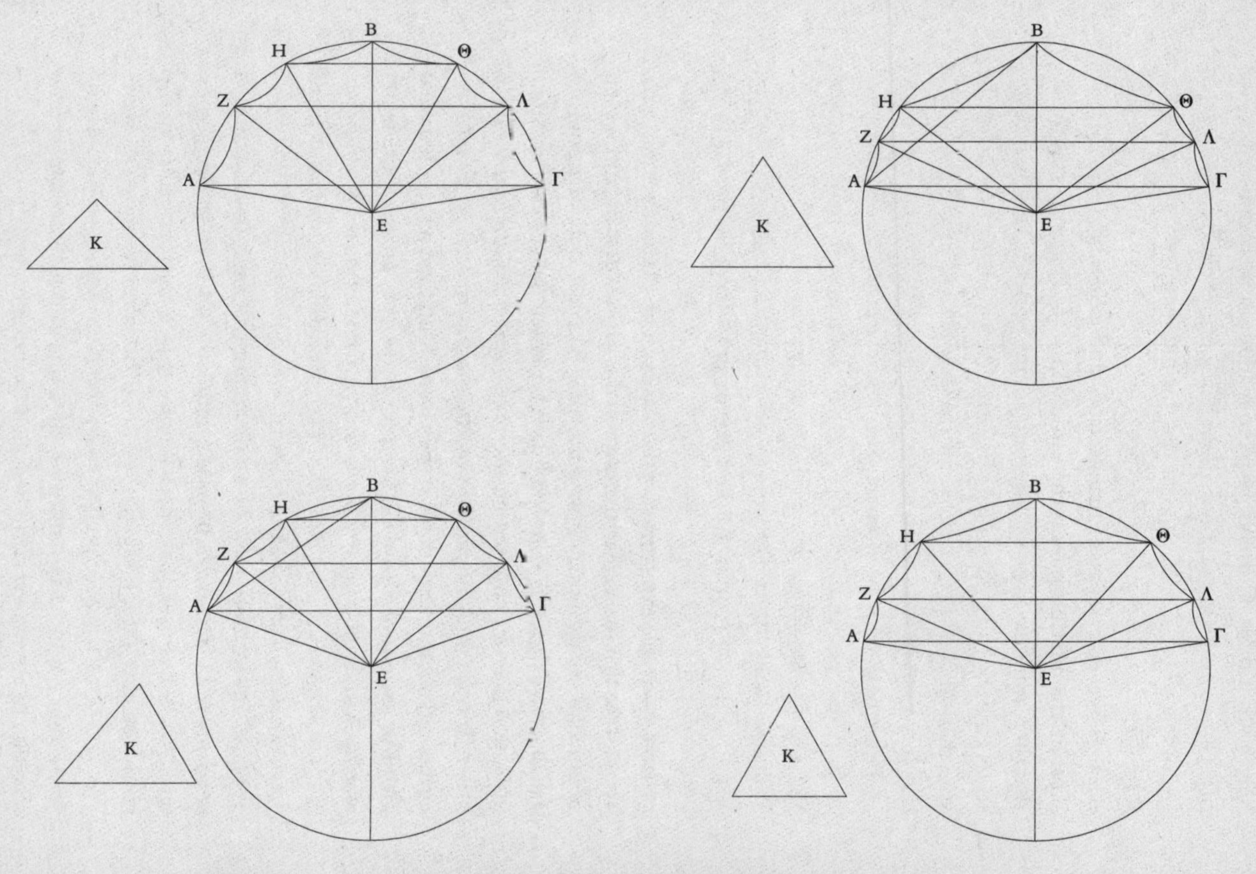

FIGURE 4.5 *Variants of diagram for* Sphere and Cylinder I, *proposition 38*

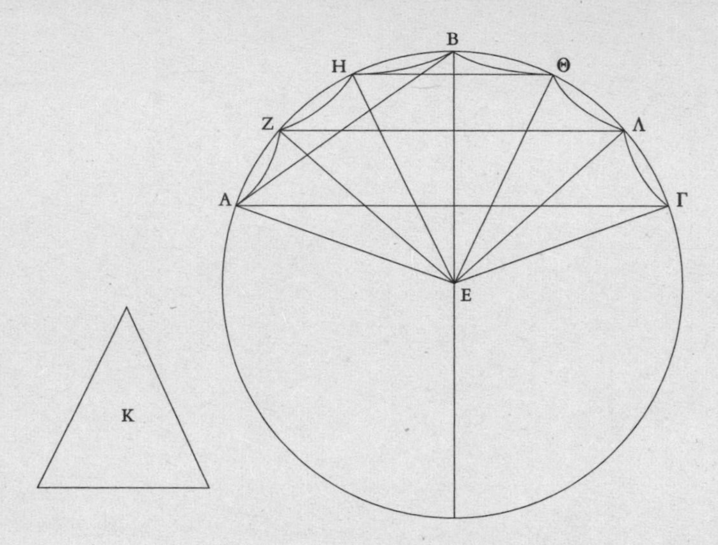

FIGURE 4.6 *Lost diagram of Codex A*

variants, I was able to reconstruct the lost diagram of Codex A (fig. 4.6). You can see that the similarity between the various descendants is such as to make my reconstruction quite safe. There is only one point of detail: two of the codices have a line AB drawn, the rest drop it. Since the line AB is not required by the text, I guess it *was* in the original figure. It was simply not copied by the more alert scribes. Two of the scribes did not think about what they were doing, and just copied what they had in front of their eyes: for this reason, they are the more trustworthy witnesses. This is a well-known paradox of the philological method, known as *lectio difficilior* ('the more difficult reading'): a bad piece of text is likely to be the original one.

Now, this in itself involves a fair amount of time travel: the descendants of Codex A are from the fifteenth and sixteenth centuries, while Codex A itself (like the Palimpsest) probably derived from the tenth century: the philological method has already gained us some 500–600 years: I have travelled from the Renaissance to the Middle Ages. But I wanted to continue my time travel. I needed a time machine to get me from the Middle Ages to antiquity.

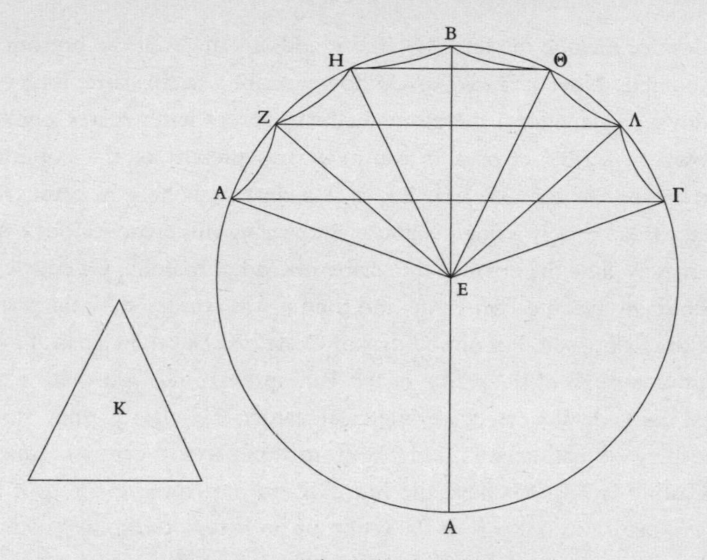

FIGURE 4.7 *The Palimpsest diagram*

The email from Will Noel inviting me to look at the Palimpsest offered just that. This was why I was so excited. I just had to look at those diagrams. Here, once again, was a crucial deciding point. Either those figures would be largely identical to those of Codex A – in which case I could reconstruct ancient diagrams; or they would be different, in which case my quest for 'the original Archimedes' would abort at around the year AD 975; Byzantine scribes – it might turn out – merely invented their diagrams and did not copy them from their originals.

And here was what I saw at Baltimore during my first visit – faintly, but the traces were familiar enough: I saw the same figure. Indeed, with digital imaging I can reconstruct this with confidence. I take the reconstructed figure from Codex A and put it side by side with the figure from the Palimpsest (see fig. 4.7). You can see that they are nearly identical. This discovery is among the most important ones made through the Palimpsest: it is the cornerstone to the reconstruction of the figures of Archimedes.

Let us continue, following the philological method. The Palimpsest does not include the line AB, and it adds a letter A at the bottom of the circle. Now, it is easy to see how a scribe can, in haste, forget to copy a single letter. I therefore chalk the absent letter A in Codex A down to scribal error and assume it was present in the common archetype. As for line AB, this is less clear: it is here in error, and since there is only a single manuscript bearing this error – Codex A – it may well be the error of the scribe of Codex A alone. Of course, it could also be an earlier error, and then it was corrected by the scribe of the Palimpsest, but not by that of Codex A. But then again, I now know enough of the scribe of the Palimpsest to tell you that he did not in general correct geometrical errors: he clearly understood nothing of mathematics, judging from some absurd errors he made. In other words, I believe the line AB was not there in front of his eyes, i.e. it was not part of the common archetype to the two codices A and the Palimpsest. And so, having completed my philological detective work, I argue that the Palimpsest preserves the ancient diagram of Archimedes' *Sphere and Cylinder I*, 38 in fig. 4.7, and we may go all the way back to Syracuse. I now move on to consider the deep conceptual significance of this.

The Logic of Greek Diagrams

Look again now at the diagram. I just said I believe it was identical to the one drawn by Archimedes himself on the sands of Syracuse. And I believe it represents the most crucial fact about Greek diagrams – one that holds the key to their great success as cognitive and logical tools. It explains why ancient diagrams did, indeed, contribute to the proof, against everything said by modern philosophers and logicians.

I need first to tell you something about the lines ΑΖΗΒΘΔΓ. In the diagram as it stands, these lines appear like a sequence of arcs, very much like the rounded edges of the drum of an ancient column. But what do they represent, geometrically? They represent a polygon – i.e. a sequence of straight lines. Indeed, in figure 4.8 you can see how

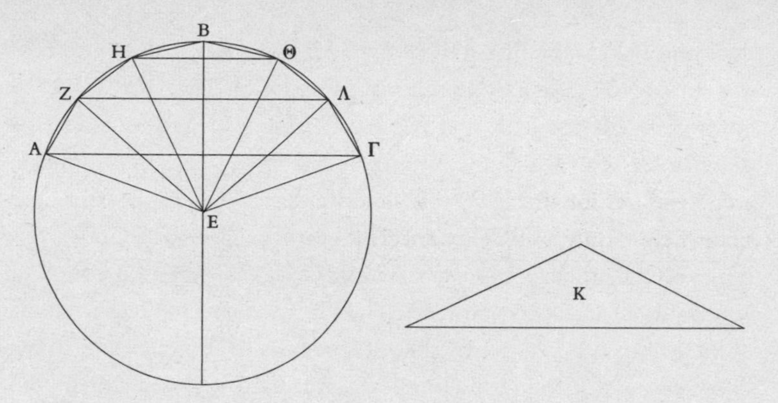

FIGURE 4.8 *A modern editor's representation of the same figure*

the modern editor has chosen to represent the same figure. Instead of arcs he has straight lines. He has preferred to call a spade a spade. If it's a polygon, let it appear like a polygon. Not so Archimedes, whose position appears to be that one may well draw a series of circular arcs to show a polygon – who cares how it looks?

This is not an isolated moment: we may compare the diagrams we could reconstruct for example for proposition 30 (see fig. 4.9) – there are altogether fourteen examples of the same type of figure in this treatise. The circular arcs form a principle of the drawings in this treatise. And it is of deep significance.

First of all, I believe no one would dare to introduce such a radical convention against the manuscript authority. Suppose you are a scribe, paid to copy diagrams from the original. The original has polygons. Well, you copy them as polygons: you do not invent circular arcs instead. And this reason – that no one would introduce such a convention against the source – can be repeated again and again, for each stage of the transmission. The only way to account for such a convention is to assume it is due to the author himself. And so this convention brings us to the shores of Syracuse – face to face with Archimedes. Let me confess: this thought does inspire me with awe. For there is something particularly 'tangible' about diagrams. Words are conceptual, drawings are physical – they are bodily. This is how

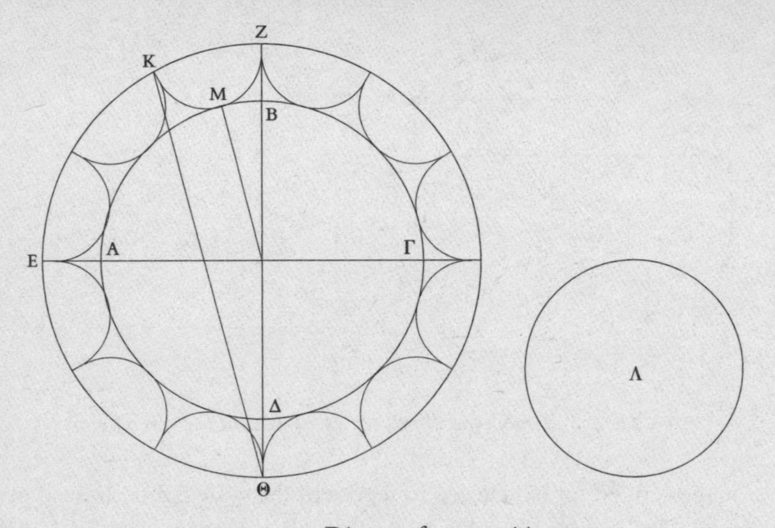

FIGURE 4.9 *Diagram for proposition 30*

he, Archimedes, traced his figure, turning a stick in his hand. If indeed I am right, and I have succeeded in reconstructing the diagrams of Archimedes, then I have reconstructed some kind of extension of his body: those are the traces left by him, personally.

And now to the next, conceptual point. What does the convention of representing polygons by circular arcs mean? It is part of a very wide phenomenon I can identify in the diagrams of Archimedes (and, indeed, in other diagrams in medieval manuscripts). Namely: the diagrams are *non-pictorial*. You draw a polygon – but you do not make your drawing look like one. Instead of being a *picture*, the ancient diagram is a *schematic representation*.

Here is another example, once again using figures from both the Palimpsest and from the modern edition. This time we look at a figure for which the only contemporary evidence is from the Palimpsest – the first figure of the *Method*, in some ways the most important piece of visual evidence contained in the Palimpsest. Of course, since we have only a single source, we can no longer apply the philological method. We cannot compare this figure to those of other medieval manuscripts, in this way deriving an original source. However, by looking elsewhere

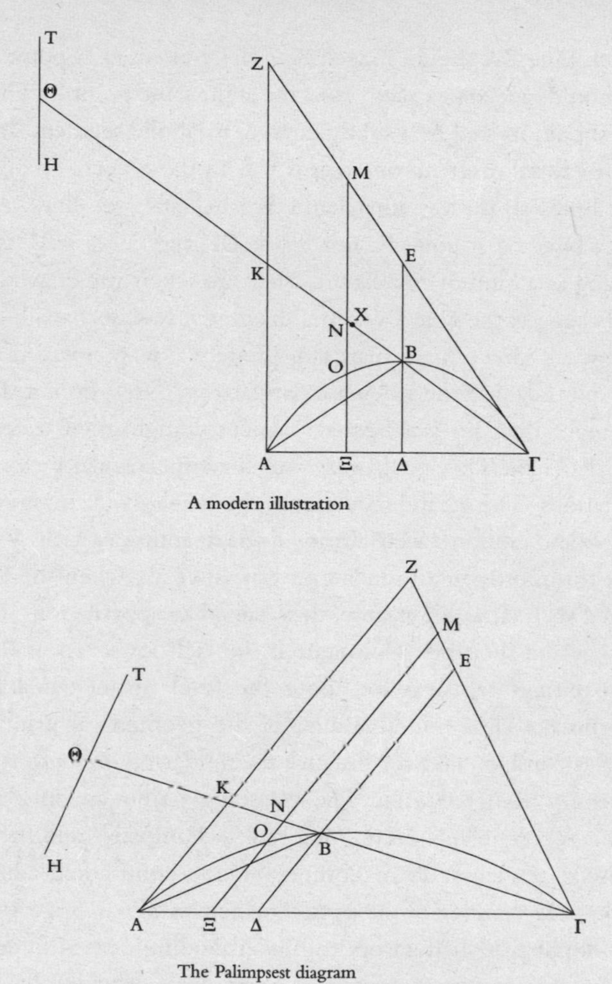

A modern illustration

The Palimpsest diagram

FIGURE 4.10 *Archimedes'* Method I

we have already gained confidence in the Palimpsest: we have seen that, whenever it could be compared to other sources, the Palimpsest contained diagrams that appear to be authentic. And so our best guess is that the diagram here, too, is close to Archimedes' original spirit.

Now, finally, compare the two drawings in figure 4.10. The modern one is 'correct'. The lines TH, ZA, etc. should indeed all be exactly parallel. Line ZA should indeed be exactly bisected at point K; ΘΓ, too, should indeed be exactly bisected at the same point K. The curve ΑΒΓ should indeed be a subtly curved, parabolic segment. In short, it is a pictorial diagram: one that is true to the object. The figure of the Palimpsest, on the other hand, is schematic: the line ZA is not exactly bisected at point K, nor is line ΘΓ; the curve ΑΒΓ is drawn freehand as a kind of circular arc. Such are schematic drawings: they merely suggest the object without drawing it precisely at all.

Why did Greek mathematicians produce non-pictorial drawings? Why did they find the schematic satisfactory? Now, do not think for a moment that this was because ancient draughtsmen were in any sense deficient. They could very well draw spectacular pictorial representations. The great discoveries of the Renaissance masters – perspective and illusion – were already made in antiquity itself. We know about this mostly in a roundabout way: after all, when the Romans pillaged such cities as Syracuse, they gained an appetite for Greek art, and they did their best to imitate it. In such lost cities as Pompeii, wall paintings tell us a lot about the level of ancient art – and they show a clear understanding of the geometrical principles of draughtsmanship. Take for instance the rendering of depth and foreshortening in figure 4.11. The vanishing points are in place; the illusion is compelling. Here, on a wall in Pompeii – and there were hundreds of such walls in Pompeii alone – one could admire the Greek understanding of the optical principles of painting. And there is no doubt that such an optical understanding existed in antiquity. We have extant several treatises in optics, one of which (by Euclid) even contains a theorem specifically on pictorial foreshortening: that a wheel, seen from the side, looks like an ellipse and not like a circle! In other words, the wheels in the wall painting from Pompeii go back to knowledge shared by Euclid himself.

Yet, paradoxically, nothing of this splendid draughtsmanship is in evidence in Greek mathematical diagrams. Greek mathematicians chose to avoid the pictorial on purpose, and instead preferred 'free', schematic figures that do not represent their object. Why is that?

FIGURE 4.11

The reason is that those strange, counter-intuitive diagrams were the solution found by Greek mathematicians to the philosophical problem of using diagrams within proofs. This is a subtle, deep point. It deserves our close attention and admiration.

Remember what the philosophical trouble was with diagrams: namely, that they were particular. You want to make a general point about triangles in general (how are triangles in general measured?). However, you can't draw a triangle in general: you must draw a particular triangle. If you happen to draw a right angle, then you might be misled into believing that the area of a triangle, in general, is the product of the smaller sides, divided by two. You come to rely on the particular properties of the particular diagram.

But is it really necessarily the case that a particular diagram suggests a particular property? This is the subtle point. I could draw a green triangle, a blue circle and a red square. But if I want to make a geometrical argument about them, I wouldn't refer to their colour. In the Western tradition we do not think of colours as geometrically significant. The colour appears to be merely incidental; it is not part of the drawing at all as far as the geometry is concerned. It is there merely because it is impossible to draw a triangle without choosing some kind of colour. Usually, of course, we use black. But this does not make our geometry 'the geometry of black figures'. Colour is simply irrelevant.

Now imagine a tradition where the same is true for such properties as the size of angle. So that, for instance, a polygon may be represented by a series of circular arcs and no one thinks that there is anything wrong. Because, you see, such properties as the precise angles are simply irrelevant: this is not what a geometrical figure represents. The precise angles are rather like the colour. So that, when we draw a right-angled green triangle it is no more right-angled than it is green. Of course, it *happens* to be right-angled – just as it *happens* to be green – but both colour and precise angle are irrelevant, are discarded by the sophisticated reader. Only a naïve child would see a 'green' triangle. And only a naïve modern reader – untrained in ancient diagrams – would see a right-angled triangle.

To put this in the most general terms: ancient diagrams are schematic, and in this way they represent the broader, *topological* features of a geometrical object. Those features are indeed general and reliable – they are just as well represented by a diagram as they are represented by language; and so, ancient diagrams can form part of the logic of an argument which is perfectly valid.

We have learned, therefore, something crucial and surprising about Archimedes' thought process, about his interfaces. He essentially relied on the visual; he used it via schematic diagrams that can be used in perfect logical rigour without danger of error based on visual evidence. When Archimedes gazed at his diagrams along the Syracusan seashore, he saw there figures largely similar to those we can reproduce today, based on the Palimpsest. And I know that what he saw there was a crucial part of his thought process: one of the most basic tools that made Greek science so successful.

Mathematics is Beautiful

It was for good reason, then, that Archimedes had a diagram put on his tomb. His reasoning inherently involved diagrams. And those diagrams were used in a clever, subtle way – very different from that

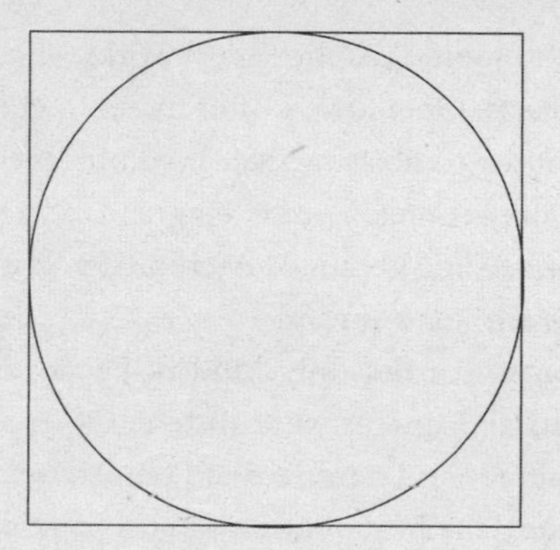

FIGURE 4.12

of modern illustrations – so that they could serve as part of the logic of the argument.

Indeed, I think I may have a guess concerning the shape of Archimedes' tomb. I think it was very simple. Greek geometrical diagrams avoid the complex effects of perspective and three-dimensional illusion. How to represent a sphere and a cylinder, then? Simply by a square enclosing a circle. I believe this may have been all there was there (perhaps with the statement, inscribed underneath, that the cylinder was one and a half the sphere). A simple, austere figure. The ancients often inscribed epigrams – short, suggestive poems of farewell and regret – upon their tombs. This diagram served as such a succinct, effective visual epigram. Perhaps it was something such as figure 4.12.

Beautiful visual epigram that it was, it would have been resonant with meaning. It would suggest many other objects, many other discoveries. The same figure of a square enclosing a circle would first of all bring to mind Archimedes' achievement of the measurement of a circle – his remarkable approximation of Π And the square and the circle could equally have suggested rectangles and parabolas, referring to Archimedes' many important discoveries concerning parabolas and other conic sections in the *Quadrature of the Parabola*, in *On Concoids and Spheroids*, in *On Floating Bodies* and, of course, in the *Method* itself. Indeed, a circle within a square would quite directly represent the theme common to most of Archimedes' works – his obsession: measuring curved objects. Of course, I offer merely a guess. Yet I find this reconstruction of the tomb attractive. It combines simplicity of form and complexity of meaning, a visual epigram and a work appropriate to the subtle story-telling genius of Archimedes. It is in this sense that Archimedes' science was beautiful.

Of course this is not the only kind of beauty one can imagine. Greek mathematical diagrams were austere. Other ancient pictures – we can once again remind ourselves of Pompeii (see fig. 4.11) – were quite the opposite. The beauty of Pompeian paintings was lavish – as no doubt was that of many mansions in Syracuse itself, in the year 212 BC. Nor is mathematics always necessarily austere. In the seventeenth century, for instance, Archimedes took a very different form. Rivault's edition of Archimedes – incidentally the one used by Newton – was produced in Paris in 1615, and it represented the rich tastes of French monarchs (to whom it was dedicated). The figures of the sphere and the cylinder were lavishly executed with the aid of three-dimensional perspective. The images of Rivault are ravishing, but they have little to do with the mathematical significance of the works of Archimedes. Indeed, by suggesting that diagrams are precise illustrations, Rivault destroys the specific achievement of ancient diagrams – their austere, abstract precision as topological, schematic drawings.

The beauty inherent in such austere drawings can be quite compelling, purely on visual grounds. Archimedes' study *Spiral Lines* is very markedly visual in this respect. Almost all of its figures are arresting, and one has the impression that Archimedes studies the spiral partly because of an aesthetic, visual fascination. The Palimpsest figure of proposition 21 (see fig. 4.13) is one of the most beautiful. (It is, of course, partly obscured by the prayer-book writing.) It is deeply austere, deeply non-pictorial. Look carefully, and you will notice that the spiral is not drawn as a true spiral, smoothly curved, but rather as a sequence of arcs of different circles. The small straight lines are especially telling – they form, indeed, the exact analogue to the curved polygons we saw in *Sphere and Cylinder*. For here, once again,

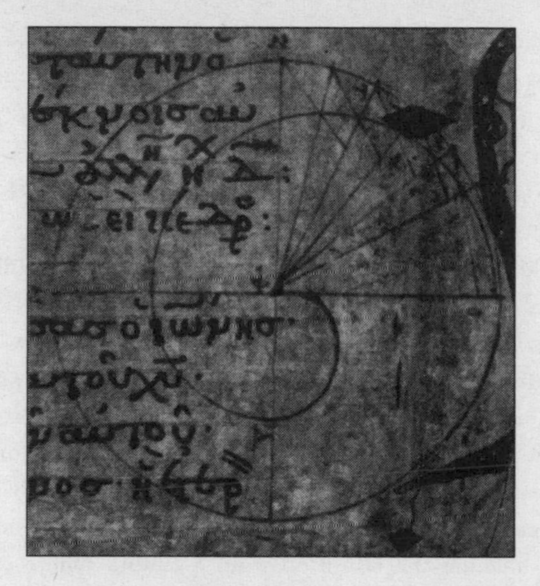

FIGURE 4.13

we see the non-pictorial character of Greek diagrams. Those small straight lines each stand for a small arc. (In *Sphere and Cylinder* arcs are drawn to represent straight lines; here, in *Spiral Lines*, straight lines are drawn to represent arcs.)

This, of course, is Archimedes of the year AD 975. It is largely faithful to the ancient Archimedes, I believe, not only in its diagrams but in its entire visual impact. The narrow columns, for instance, are significant: they hark back to the writing on papyrus rolls (which were written in a sequence of very narrow columns). As mentioned, we have no exact parallel to compare with from antiquity itself, but there are, of course, a number of scientific works that have survived in papyrus form. They are not as important as those by Archimedes or by Euclid, but still they tell us a lot about the appearance of ancient science. The earliest of them all is a very minor astronomical text, known as the *Ars Eudoxi*, which is extant in Paris, kept at the Louvre Museum, where it is known simply as 'Pap. Gr. 1', i.e. Greek papyrus number one. It is a very ancient piece of papyrus indeed – from the late third century BC, so that, possibly, this piece of papyrus could have been inscribed while Archimedes was still alive. Its narrow columns, rough, schematic figures, and its clean and yet unornamented writing are all suggestive of what we have since learned about the manuscript tradition of Archimedes himself. I believe this is what ancient science looked like.

It would not have been in book form, of course. As Will Noel has mentioned, this would be the major difference from the Palimpsest: ancient writings took the form of a roll, not a book. Instead of leafing through Archimedes, you would roll him out. Will has pointed out how inconvenient this is for extracting information from, say, a dictionary. But I think the roll is, in fact, quite handy for the continuous reading of geometry. The reason Will is right is that, at about the time people were making the transition from roll to codex, they were also making the transition from a culture where continuous reading mattered most to one where extraction of information was paramount. This has now come to be the world of the ultimate reference work – the Bible.

The roll is more convenient for geometry, as the following consideration suggests. Did you ever read a piece of geometry that extended beyond a couple of pages? You will recall the experience, then, of leafing back and forth while you were reading, from text to diagram and back, forgetting the diagram while reading the text and then forgetting the text while reading the diagram. The roll is in this respect a much better interface. (I say, geometrical books should be printed on rolls!) You roll out the book so that you have in front of your eyes, perfectly, the entire text together with the figure. Such was the ancient mathematical roll: a polished piece of spare design. Think of it as the equivalent of an elegant Italian coffee machine: simple lines joined together to make a perfect product.

The simplicity would be not only in the drawings but also in the writing itself. This is a major consideration in the history of writing – not only for mathematics but for any writing whatsoever. In time, writing diversifies. Ancient writing was simpler than ours: instead of the many fonts we use, and especially instead of the division we have between upper-case and lower-case characters, the ancients knew just one font, just one case – effectively, the upper one. THIS IS WHAT ANCIENT WRITING LOOKED LIKE. This is what the *Ars Eudoxi* looks like, and this is how Archimedes' original writings looked. Which is simple and elegant, in its own way.

As writing gets diversified, the interface changes. In the Middle Ages – i.e., in the Palimpsest – the writing used to copy Archimedes would already have been different. And this, too, is important for the history of mathematical interfaces. I have already said that, today, the emblem of mathematics is the equation, the arrangement of symbols. And this is the product of a long historical process whose roots lie in the Middle Ages. For this, once again, let us turn to the Archimedes Palimpsest.

The Medieval Origins of Mathematical Symbols

The Palimpsest is an important piece of evidence not only for the year 225 BC but also for the year AD 975. The scribe who put down the works of Archimedes perhaps did not do much to advance the concepts of mathematics. He was no Archimedes. In point of fact, I am sure this scribe knew no mathematics at all. But he necessarily made a contribution to the history of the *interfaces* of mathematics. His choices in the manner of writing down the words, arranging them on the page and putting the works together all made a contribution to the way Archimedes would be read by later mathematicians. This is true through history, all the way from Archimedes in Syracuse down to the present day: scribes, typesetters and publishers make a silent contribution to the history of science, sometimes as important as that of the scientists themselves.

And so scribes have, silently, invented the mathematical symbol. In this they prepared the way for the modern equation, the most powerful tool of modern science. While faithfully copying Archimedes'

FIGURE 4.14 Sphere and Cylinder II*: a phrase from proposition 2*

diagrams, the scribe from the year 975 was already preparing the way for the equations of today's science.

Let us look at a passage from the Palimpsest. Figure 4.14 is from the second proposition of the second book on *Sphere and Cylinder.* Just as we saw for Greek diagrams, the writing, in the original Greek produced by Archimedes, had no frills at all. ARCHIMEDES WROTE LIKE THIS, or, more precisely, ARCHIMEDESWROTELIKETHIS (word division, too, is a medieval invention). In particular, Archimedes' text had no abbreviations: he spelled every word out fully.

A scribe's work, though, is very tedious: copying out, word after word, character after character. It just makes so much more sense to abbreviate. If a word is repeated very often, why not invent a symbol to represent this word directly, instead of copying it out again and again? Of course there are aesthetic disadvantages to that. With too many abbreviations the text may no longer look like Greek and begin to look like stenography. With a work of poetry, say, produced for a high price, you would not use many abbreviations. But a technical work such as mathematics was probably not very highly paid. The

Archimedes Palimpsest is an example of a fine, polished piece of scribal craftsmanship, but it is not a luxury manuscript. No one would stop the scribe from using scribal abbreviations.

And so we go back to the text of *Sphere and Cylinder*. Here is a translation of his text:

> (1) Therefore as the [line] KΘ to the [line] ΘE, the [line] ΘE to [the line] EΓ, and therefore as the [square] on KΔ to the [rectangle contained] by KΘΔ, the [square] on AΓ to the [rectangle contained] by AEΓ

You will notice first of all that my English translation takes up much more space than the Greek text in the manuscript. There are two reasons for this, one due to Archimedes, another to the medieval scribes. The first is those square brackets. Archimedes does not write in such words as 'line', 'square', 'rectangle', letting the reader infer them from the context. In this way he is capable of writing a very spare text. The language used by Archimedes is a piece of polished, minimalist design, on a par with his skeletal, polished diagrams. He can use very few words – because the readers already know what kinds of things he is talking about (just as the readers can 'read' the minimalist diagrams correctly, because they understand their nature as *mathematical* diagrams). Since Archimedes used only upper-case letters, and no word divisions, his text looked like this:

> (2)THEREFOREASTHETKΘTOTHEΘETHEΘETOEΓAND THEREFOREASTHEONKΔTOTHEBYKΘΔTHEONAΓTO THEBYAEΓ

This, indeed, is somewhat challenging as an interface.

Medieval scribes, at this point, took some crucial steps in the invention of more effective typesetting interfaces. The use of several cases – an upper case alongside a lower case – is of great value. It allows us to separate the letters referring to the diagram (which remain in upper case) from the rest (which is now in lower case). Word division is another major invention. The two together bring us to a text that is more familiar to us:

> (3) Therefore as the KΘ to the ΘE, the ΘE to EΓ, and therefore as the on KΔ to the by KΘΔ, the on AΓ to the by AEΓ

At this point the medieval scribes introduced yet another major invention – their own contribution to making the text so compact. They introduced abbreviations. They did not do this because of any deep, sophisticated mathematical reason. They did this because they were *lazy*. And so, instead of copying out the word *pros* (the Greek for 'to') time and again, they simply inserted a symbol that looked somewhat like our capital sigma, Σ. There are other abbreviations or symbols, such as for 'as' (a bit like *w*), for 'and' (a bit like *K*) and 'therefore' (a bit like ϵ), all marked in figure 4.14. So this is what the text finally looks like:

> (4) ϵ *w* the KΘ Σ the ΘE, the ΘE Σ EΓ, *K* ϵ *w* the on KΔ Σ the by KΘΔ, the on AΓ Σ the by AEΓ

Note also that the Greek word 'the' can often be written out in one or two characters (it changes according to gender and case), instead of the three characters of English 'the'. I represent this by an abbreviation, *t'*, to allow us to get a full flavour of the original writing:

> (5) ϵ *w t'* KΘ Σ *t'* ΘE, *t'* ΘE Σ EΓ, *K* ϵ *w t'* on KΔ Σ*t'* by KΘΔ, *t'* on AΓ Σ *t'* by AEΓ

This, too, may well appear rather confusing, and you may even prefer the full form of example (1) above to the abbreviations of example (5). You may feel that example (5) is written out in hieroglyphics. But this is all a matter of habit: one simply needs to learn this particular notation – the way we learn our own modern notations. For instance, a modern mathematician may well put down the same text as follows:

> (6) ➔ KΘ:ΘE::ΘE:EΓ
> ➔ $K\Delta^2$:KΘ★ΘΔ::$A\Gamma^2$:AE★EΓ

which is exactly as hieroglyphic as example (5). Archimedes himself would have had no idea what example (6) was talking about, just as a modern reader, faced with example (5), has no idea what this is about. One has to learn the notation – and then the hieroglyphs make perfect sense as a symbolic rendering of the contents.

For this is the deep point. All the examples – from (1) to (6) – contain *exactly* the same meaning, merely changing the packaging. The difference is in the interface. But what a difference an interface makes! Indeed, the invention of abbreviated notations is one of the key steps in the growth of modern science.

The history of this invention still needs to be charted. Scholars have only very recently started to look at medieval manuscripts not as containers of information about antiquity but as interesting documents in their own right. How did scribes come to invent a system such as that of example (5)? We still do not know the full answer; we are still collecting the evidence. As the earliest extant manuscript of Archimedes, the Palimpsest will form one of the key pieces of evidence for this research.

The broad outlines of this history – the history of the scientific interface – are, however, clear. The transition was made from the science of diagrams to the science of equations. Indeed, these may be seen as two different ways of utilising human visual skills within this highly conceptual field of mathematical thought. From one kind of visual science – the Greek one based on the diagram – we have made the transition to another kind of visual science – the modern one based on the symbol and the equation.

The Archimedes Palimpsest stands midway: as the best evidence we can gain, indirectly, on the old science of diagrams; and as a major piece of evidence for the new (then nascent) science of symbols and equations.

The Mathematical Experience

Everything I have referred to – the nature of the mathematical diagram, the beauty of the mathematical page, the invention of mathematical symbolism – everything leads to a single point: mathematics is a matter of experience. Of course, mathematics is a highly conceptual, abstract discipline. But even an abstract content has to be mastered by a human person, somehow. It has to be sensed through the eyes. As humans, we are capable of understanding abstract concepts, but we can only understand them via our experience. The most abstract concepts must have some sensual packaging, in the sounds of language and in the artefacts of vision. For humans, to understand is, first of all, to see and to hear.

Such is the emerging consensus, in recent decades, among philosophers, logicians, historians and cognitive scientists: cognition and logic, the abstract and the concrete, are ultimately inseparable. Which, in a sense, is something palaeographers – the scholars of ancient writing – knew all along.

In the study of ancient manuscripts one is used to such questions as: How is the text written? What are the visual tools invented by the scribe? How is the page meant to work? When studying a manuscript, one is led to a study of both content and form. The ideas conveyed by the text may be abstract, but their setting out in physical form is not. This is indeed a physical object – as Will Noel calls it: Archimedes' brain in a box. This is the purpose of it all: by the study of the cognitive history of diagrams and symbols, of pages and manuscripts, that we may gain an understanding of Archimedes' own brain – as it worked back then, at Syracuse.

Only that, when I met Will Noel in the spring of 1999, one could barely glimpse any of this evidence. The manuscript made in 975 had been nearly obliterated by the millennium separating us from Byzantium's heyday. It is time to rejoin John Dean and Will Noel in their journey across the Mediterranean in order to understand how this came to pass – how this manuscript was changed beyond recognition; and yet, time and again, managed, against the odds, to survive.

5

The Great Race, Part II
The History of the Palimpsest

Disaster Strikes

Back in Constantinople, John Dean and I climbed up the Galata Tower and looked out. Beyond the Golden Horn the glorious panorama of Constantinople was spread before us. Hagia Sophia and the Blue Mosque dominated the view. The mosque was a reminder that Constantinople fell to the Ottoman Turks in 1453. This is often heralded as a great tragedy, but the really disastrous sack of Constantinople had already happened 250 years earlier. It was perpetrated by Christians from Western Europe.

In 1204 the Fourth Crusade, sanctioned by Pope Innocent III, had to get from Europe to Egypt, and from there, in theory, to the Holy Land. The problem was how to get to Egypt. The Doge of Venice was prepared to provide a fleet for 4,000 knights, 9,000 squires and 20,000 foot soldiers, but at the price of 86,000 marks. The crusaders agreed, but they were 34,000 marks short when they were ready to sail. So they agreed to recapture the Dalmatian city of Zara for the Venetians and their part of the loot would make up the difference. The crusaders trashed Zara, but after they had pillaged the town their loot was still not enough to pay the debt. The crusaders could not, in honour, default on their debt to the Doge. There was an imperative to recover it. How to do this? Politics supplied the answer. Isaac II, Emperor of Constantinople, had been ousted by Alexius II in 1195, blinded and thrown into a dungeon. Isaac's daughter was married to

Philip of Swabia, and his son, Alexius Angelus, was also at Philip's court. Alexius Angelus agreed to pay the crusaders and the Doge of Venice 200,000 marks if they would install him on the throne of Constantinople. The Pope would be happy because Alexius Angelus agreed that the city would become Catholic; the Doge would be happy because he would get his money and trading privileges, and the powerful Philip of Swabia would have a puppet on the throne of Constantinople. Even modern politics doesn't get much grubbier than this.

The realities of medieval conquest do. The crusaders succeeded in toppling Alexius II without even taking the city, and Alexius Angelus was made co-emperor with his father Isaac II. But even with their puppet in place, the debt remained, and Constantinople was in no position to pay the money that Alexius had promised. While the crusaders were waiting for it, a few of them started attacking a mosque. A fire broke out in the chaos that followed. It spread very quickly and soon great tracts of the city stood in flames. The fire lasted for eight days, killing hundreds and destroying a strip three miles wide running right through the middle of the ancient city. Still the money was not forthcoming. Alexius, not surprisingly, lost the support of the beleaguered inhabitants; he was strangled, and his father Isaac II died of grief. Hostilities broke out again. On Monday, 12 April 1204 the crusaders breached the ancient walls of Theodosius. That same night another great fire broke out, destroying further parts of the ancient city. The next day Constantinople surrendered. But it was only then that the full horror, the horror recorded first hand by Nicetas Choniates, began. As a result, the cash went into the coffers of the Doge, the city went into the hands of the crusaders, the Catholic faith was imposed upon the Orthodox, and the classics went up in flames.

This was truly a cataclysmic event for the texts of the ancient world. The ark of the classics was burned. This is how fully twenty of the thirty-three historians discussed by Photius disappeared. Who knows how many copies of Archimedes' treatises? The future of these treatises was not in Constantinople. The copies that survived in the thirteenth century were to be found elsewhere. Codices A, B and C were flotsam upon the waters of the Mediterranean world. Let's see where they washed up – first Codices A and B, and then C, the book on my desk.

Archimedes in Italy

In 1881 a scholar named Valentin Rose came across a manuscript in the great Vatican Library. It was written by William of Moerbeke, a Franciscan friar and a great translator of Greek texts, including several works of Aristotle. But this was his translation of the works of Archimedes, from the Greek into Latin. He finished writing this book on Tuesday, 10 December 1269. Since William became a chaplain and penitentiary of Pope Clement IV at Viterbo, in Italy, some time in the 1260s and was still there in 1271, it must have been at Viterbo that he translated Archimedes' treatises.

But what were the manuscripts that William translated from, and where did he get them? There were two of them, and they are both listed in a catalogue of manuscripts belonging to the Pope in 1311. These were the manuscripts that we call Codex A and Codex B. Number 612 was Codex A. Even in 1269 it cannot have been in great shape, because it was missing its cover. In the catalogue, the codex is recorded as Angevin. This probably means that it was given to the Pope by Charles I of Anjou, after the Battle of Benevento in 1266. Number 608 was Codex B. Since Codex A did not contain *Floating Bodies*, William translated it from this second manuscript.

So Codices A and B washed up in Italy. But Codex B didn't last very long; it hasn't been seen since 1311. Codex A, on the other hand, became one of the most highly sought after codices of the Italian Renaissance. In 1450 it was in the hands of Pope Nicholas V, who commissioned Jacopo of Cremona to translate it again. In 1492 Lorenzo de Medici – Il Magnifico – sent Politian on a search for texts that he didn't have in his library. Politian found Codex A in the library of Giorgio Valla in Venice, and he had a copy of it made. This copy is now housed in Michelangelo's architectural masterpiece, the Laurentian Library in Florence. Valla thought Codex A so precious and rare that he would not let it out of his library and even declined a request to borrow it from Ercole d'Este, Duke of Ferrara. Alberto Pio of Carpi bought Giorgio Valla's library. When Pio died, in 1531, the manuscript came into the possession of his nephew Ridolfo Pio, who died in 1564. No one has seen Codex A since then.

Even though they disappeared, Codices A and B did their job: they transmitted Archimedes to the modern world. The reception of Archimedes has been meticulously documented in the monumental work of scholarship by Marshall Clagett, *Archimedes in the Middle Ages*. Whether it was directly through Codex A or through the Latin translations of William of Moerbeke and Jacopo of Cremona, Archimedes' treatises came into the hands of the most talented men of the Renaissance. The Renaissance was, of course, well disposed to receiving the works of this great man.

The Archimedes of legend had already become a byword for brilliant inventors and mathematicians. Filippo Brunelleschi, for example, was heralded as a 'Second Archimedes' for building the magnificent dome of Florence Cathedral early in the fifteenth century. But the Archimedes that Renaissance men found in the treatises was quite the match of the legendary figure. Leon Battista Alberti, the great Florentine author, architect and painter, knew of *Floating Bodies* and applied it to his exposition of the '*Eureka*' story. More impressively, as James Banker showed in 2005, Piero della Francesca, whose paintings reveal astonishing subtleties of geometry, actually transcribed the full text of Jacopo of Cremona's translation. And Regiomontanus, the German mathematician whose work was so important to Copernicus, also copied Jacopo's translation after the Pope had given it to Cardinal Bessarion. By hook or by crook the great artistic and mathematical minds of the Renaissance got their hands on Archimedes' treatises. And it became significantly easier for them to do this after 1544, for in that year, in Basle, the first edition of the works of Archimedes was printed. For many of his treatises, the race against destruction was over, and they had won. Galileo and Newton read them, and modern science was born.

The Book Leonardo Never Knew

It might strike you that I have left out one of the greatest minds of the Renaissance in my list: Leonardo da Vinci. We have seen that, from Hero onwards, Archimedes was of interest to the foremost mathematicians and architects of their day – people who could not only master higher mathematics but who also wanted to apply their knowledge. It is no surprise, therefore, that Leonardo, too, was anxious to get hold of copies of Archimedes' works. In his notebook he writes: 'A complete Archimedes is in the hands of the brother of the Monsignor of Santa Giusta in Rome. He said that it had been given to his brother who was in Sardinia. It was first in the library of the Duke of Urbino but was taken away at the time of Duke Valentino.' Somehow Leonardo must have succeeded in getting hold of some Archimedes manuscripts. His notebooks reveal knowledge of the *Measurement of the Circle*, *Spiral Lines*, *Sphere and Cylinder*, *Floating Bodies*, and *Balancing Planes*. The last named of these treatises particularly fascinated Leonardo, because it concerned finding centres of gravity. Leonardo used it to show how to find the centre of gravity in a triangle. (In the next chapter, with Reviel, you will be doing the same.) Being Leonardo, he did not stop with what he could discover from Archimedes. He used Archimedes' work as a platform for his own calculations. You see, in *Balancing Planes*, Archimedes only discussed how to find the centre of gravity in plane figures. Leonardo went beyond this and tried to find centres of gravity in solid ones too, all the time by applying Archimedes' own techniques. And he did come up with a theorem for finding the centre of gravity in a tetrahedron. It was a remarkable achievement by this Renaissance giant and typical of the way in which Renaissance scholars built on the work of Archimedes.

But there was one treatise that Leonardo did not know about. Consequently, he could not have known that Archimedes had, 1,700 years earlier, already gone way beyond him. In the *Method*, Archimedes had already found the centres of gravity for much more complicated solids than the tetrahedron – solids with curved surfaces. In his letter to Eratosthenes, Archimedes had calculated the centre of gravity for a paraboloid, a spherical segment, a segment of an ellipsoid, and even a segment of a hyperboloid. It's not that Leonardo researched his subject inadequately. Leonardo couldn't have known this text. It wasn't part of Codex A or Codex B, the only two Greek manuscripts by which Archimedes was known to the Renaissance. It was part of Codex C. Or rather, it had been.

A Write-off

A scribe prepared himself for a job. He had gone through these procedures many times before. He had already prepared his reed pens; he had his ruler and his knife. He sat down in a chair. Beside him was a small table with an inkwell filled with black ink. He took the first sheet of parchment from a stack nearby. With a hard point he incised lines on the parchment upon which he would shortly write his letters (to do this he used a straight edge, which he aligned with small holes pricked on the edges of the folios). The parchment now rested in his lap on top of a board. In front of the scribe, on a stand, was the codex that he was about to copy. He was poised to write. Are you experiencing déjà vu? Excellent. Look at the scene again. This time we are not particularly interested in the codex on the stand. It is the parchment that the scribe is about to use that should be the object of our curiosity. It was going through a process it had been through before.

You have guessed, of course. This scribe's parchment was Codex C, the Archimedes manuscript from *Balancing Planes* to *Stomachion*,

FIGURE 5.1 *How to make a palimpsest*

Method included, but now taken apart and its folios erased of text. The scribe had more prayers to write than he had Archimedes parchment to write on, but this didn't stop him. He simply re-used parchment from other codices as well – at least four of them.

The palimpsesting of Archimedes, and of all the unidentified texts now in the prayer book, was a ruthless operation. The manuscripts were taken from their shelves, their bindings were cut off and discarded, and the stitching between their quires was undone. This was quick and easy to do. Once the codex was in pieces, the bifolios were scrubbed with some kind of natural acid. There are no Greek texts telling us how this was done, but Theophilus, writing *On Various Arts* in Western Europe in the twelfth century, suggests that by using orange juice and a sponge it is quite easy to erase letters perfectly. No doubt some kind of acidic mixture was used, but the operation on the Palimpsest was much more severe than the one prescribed by Theophilus. Abigail found holes on the edges of the Archimedes bifolios that appear to have been made by nails which held them under tension. This would be consistent with the damp bifolios being tacked down to a board, as they would have shrunk as they dried out. Abigail further noticed that there were scratch marks over the top of the Archimedes text: after the bifolios had dried, they were further rubbed with a pumice stone. There you are: it's done. Having been crucified most effectively, the skins on which Archimedes' texts were written were taken down from their wooden frames and stacked in a corner.

The first thing the scribe did upon picking up an Archimedes bifolio was to cut it in two down the fold, and so separate it into two folios. He did not trim these folios further, and this is lucky: it means that, on each surviving folio, none of the residual traces of the Archimedes text were trimmed off by the maker of the palimpsest. He then took the two folios, rotated them ninety degrees and folded them in the middle so that they became two nested bifolios in the prayer book. Folios of the prayer book are therefore exactly half the size of the original Archimedes folios.

However, when the scribe picked up separate Archimedes bifolios, these bifolios were already highly disordered, so different bifolios of the Archimedes text are now found widely separated from each other in the prayer book. They are also found interspersed with palimpsested parchment of the other manuscripts that the scribe used. The Archimedes manuscript formed the overall skeleton of the Palimpsest; the parchment of other manuscripts fleshed it out.

It made good sense for the scribe to cut the bifolios in half and rotate them, and this was standard practice in palimpsests. The great advantage of this procedure was that scribes did not have to contend with the distracting remains of a palimpsested text because they were writing at right angles to it. It is far easier to write over a text at right angles than it is to follow its path. Of course, the scribe could have simply rotated the scrubbed bifolios, without cutting them down the middle, and folded them in half the other way. But then they would have made an extremely tall, thin and unwieldy codex. The procedure followed by our scribe was carefully designed to produce new codices effectively and economically. For this reason, palimpsested codices are nearly always half the size of the codices from which they were made. Of course, since a folio of the Archimedes manuscript became a bifolio of the prayer book, it could, and often did, constitute both the first and last folio of a quire in the new manuscript. As a result the middle of each of the old Archimedes folios passed right through the spine of the prayer book.

If he knew what he was about to copy over, the scribe did not give it a second thought. His first piece of parchment in his new codex contained *On Floating Bodies*. He covered it with a blessing for loaves at Easter. A little later on he wrote over a different section with a prayer for repentance. He wrote over the beginning of the *Method* with a prayer of marriage. Over a later section of the *Method* he wrote a prayer said at the foundation of a church, and – note this – over proposition 14 he wrote a prayer for the dead.

For a short section of the prayer book our scribe worked together with a colleague. He was probably glad of the help, as it was a long job. Since no one who had investigated the Archimedes Palimpsest was very interested in these codices, it is entirely appropriate that over a folio of one of them the scribes wrote a prayer for those unreasonably excluded.

Good sense it may have been, but the scribes of the prayer book had really stitched up Archimedes. Think about it. If some odd duck ever wanted, for some strange reason, to read any one of the palimpsested texts, it would be great fun to watch them try. For example, if someone was interested in the text of *Method*, proposition 14, they would have trouble finding it. It started on column 1 of folio 110 recto of the Palimpsest. To read it, they would have to turn the codex ninety degrees and read through the prayer book text – the prayer for the dead – to decipher the erased text beneath. Very soon they would get stuck, as the column disappeared into the gutter. They would have to find where it reappeared – in this case five folios further back, on folio 105v. They would not be able to read at least two of the lines of text hidden in the gutter. If they persisted, they would have to read the second column of text too. Here things get more complicated. They would have to rotate the codex 180 degrees and read column 1 of folio 110v, and rotate it 180 degrees again to read the bottom of this column on folio 105r. To finish with this folio, they would have to repeat this operation. Having read as much of this folio as they could, they would then need to find the next folio of Archimedes text. It could be anywhere in the codex. Actually it was on folio 158, more than fifty folios further on. Then the whole process would start again. A truly interactive user experience. But nobody would ever do this, would they? I mean, it's a mug's game.

So what was the name of the ignorant Christian who did this? And what, if any, are the mitigating circumstances that the defence can summon up before we pass judgement on him for obliterating Archimedes? Having no idea how to answer these questions, I roundly condemn an anonymous medieval ignoramus, and move on. The book moved on, too, and when we can trace it next, it is three hundred years later and on a different continent.

Buried in the Desert

John Dean and I left Constantinople behind and flew to the Holy Land. We arrived in Tel Aviv, hired a car and headed for Jerusalem. We went to the Wailing Wall – the foundations of Solomon's Temple. We saw the Dome of the Rock – where the prophet Muhammad ascended to Heaven and met with Allah. We visited the Church of the Holy Sepulchre – where Christ was buried. The next day we headed south out of Jerusalem, past the security checkpoint, into the West Bank, and a different world. We drove to Bethlehem, and got lost. We couldn't find our turning, and we couldn't speak Arabic. John's smile was a sign of friendship and my agitation an international signal of distress. The combination persuaded a very patient Palestinian to get us back on the right road.

We turned left, to the east, and to the desert. The road ended and we got out of the car. It was the early evening and the sun was low in the sky, but it was extraordinarily dry and hot. To our left a boy on a donkey passed us, whacking his stick and driving his goats back to the village. Apart from the bells around the necks of the animals it was silent. We could see for miles across the Judaean desert. The sky was blue over Jordan; the land, everywhere, was burnt ochre. Below, about a mile further down a gravel path, I saw two towers. I had seen them before, in black and white, in a nineteenth-century engraving above the desk of my friend Patrick Zutshi in Cambridge. They looked exactly the same, and I knew them to be the towers of the Monastery of St Sabas.

The print I knew was by the Royal Academician David Roberts. He had arrived at the Monastery on Thursday, 4 April 1839, together with the Reverend George Croly. They had initially approached the monastery from a different angle, from the east. Croly records:

> The immediate approach to the convent is striking . . . It was night when after having descended into the bed of a ravine, where the Kidron passes to the Dead Sea, and arriving at the foot of the Mountain of St Saba, we saw the convent above us, by the uncertain light of the moon. It looked a lofty and colossal structure, rising in stories and terraces, one above another, against the sides of the mountain to its summit, and there crowned with clouds. An old white-bearded monk, leaning on his staff, was toiling up the side of the hill leading a long procession of devotees. Below, apparently growing out of the rock, was a large palm tree said to have been planted by the hands of the Saint in the fourth century. History, and probably legend, contributed its share to the effect. In a chapel behind an iron grating in one of the grottos was a pile of skulls. The tradition of the convent said they were those of hermits who, to the amount of several thousand, had been slaughtered by the Osmanlis [i.e. Ottomans]. We ascended the flight of steps, climbed up a ladder, crept through a small door only large enough to admit one at a time, and found ourselves in an antechamber, surrounded by above a hundred Greek pilgrims . . . It was Passion Week. The monks receive strangers with courtesy, and they not merely permitted the artist to sketch their chapel, but as their service was beginning before he had finished his design, they would not suffer him to lay aside his pencil.

John and I went through the main door, which was in a round archway and painted deep blue. We were received warmly by the only monk in the community of thirteen who admitted to speaking English. His given name was Lazarus, and he had come to the monastery from San Francisco. He showed us around the complex, the cell of St Sabas himself, and the chapel of St Nicholas, wherein are indeed housed the skulls of the departed members of the community. It is still a most extraordinary, beautiful and spiritual place, despite the political upheavals that constantly surround it. Everything was as Croly had described it, and time melted away. Brother Lazarus had found peace in St Sabas. He missed the Grateful Dead, but he was reminded of them by the insistent ringing of the semantron, a crescent-shaped metal bar by which a fellow monk was even then calling him to prayer. Before he left us he pointed to the taller of two towers that crowned the assemblage of churches and cells, St Justinian's Tower, and he said that it contained the library. John and I had reached our destination. In 1834 there were more than 1,000 manuscripts in the library of St Sabas. One of them, one of the least prepossessing, was the Archimedes Palimpsest.

We only know that the Archimedes Palimpsest was at St Sabas because when a Greek scholar called Papadopoulos-Kerameus described the manuscript in 1899, he said that there was in the book an added paper quire from the sixteenth century, and on one of these leaves, folio 184, was an inscription indicating that the book belonged to the monastery. The manuscript doesn't have 184 folios any more, and this inscription no longer exists. It is only thanks to Papadopoulos-Kerameus that we know how the Archimedes Palimpsest survived the centuries.

The Palimpsest contains prayers that the brothers in the monastery could use on an almost daily basis: there is a prayer that you say when something unclean falls into a vessel of wine, oil or honey; there is St Gregory's exorcism for unclean spirits and John Chrysostom's prayer for Holy Communion, to name just a few of them. The Palimpsest shows every sign of the uses to which it was put. The codex is charred at the edges, as if it has been scorched by the desert heat or even burned in a fire, and many of the folios are covered with wax droplets, which would have fallen on the manuscript as its prayers were recited by candlelight. There are many emendations and additions to the text, and in some places the prayer-book text itself has been written over to make it more legible. Moreover, either through damage, or because its prayers were no longer considered relevant, approximately sixty folios from the manuscript went missing while it was at St Sabas. That is about a third of the entire codex.

The Monastery of St Sabas provided temporary respite for John and me, and a more permanent sanctuary for Brother Lazarus. But it was a tomb for Archimedes. The monks had every reason to use the prayers in the Palimpsest, but absolutely none to read what was beneath them. Abstract mathematics is not a priority in St Sabas. Archimedes was buried effectively at the monastery for at least three hundred years. Unlike the texts in Codices A and B, those unique to Codex C remained unknown to the Renaissance and the Scientific Revolution. Somehow, like Brother Lazarus's biblical namesake, the Archimedes of the *Method* and *Stomachion* would have to be raised from the dead.

Signs of Movement

One of the last stops on my journey with John Dean was Lincoln College, Oxford, to see a great scholar and a gentleman, Nigel Wilson. I have already spoken of Nigel, because in talking about the transmission of ancient texts to modern times you have to. But it was only when I met him in Oxford that I got to know him at all. The first thing that struck me was that he was honoured to meet us. This was only in part impeccable civility. It was mainly because I bore responsibility for the Palimpsest, work on which he was later to describe as 'one of the most fascinating scholarly projects imaginable'. The Palimpsest really mattered to Nigel, and this also accounted for his remarkable patience when we filmed him over and over again in the college library, repeating some of the simplest statements that he has ever contrived to utter. One sound bite he gave us was: 'Constantinople was the one place in the ancient world with an unbroken tradition of copying and studying ancient texts.' Another was: 'I went to Cambridge, saw the leaf and said, "That's it: that's Archimedes."'

In truth, in 1971, and acting on a suggestion of his friend G. J. Toomer of Brown University, Nigel had set out from Oxford to Cambridge to see a palimpsest fragment that had been catalogued by Pat Easterling as containing a mathematical text. Nigel found it easy to read, and he recognised from a technical term that this was Archimedes. Indeed it came from *Sphere and Cylinder*, and it fitted between folios 2 and 3 of the Palimpsest.

The fragment was in Cambridge University Library, and it had the number Add. 1879.23. The University Library logs its acquisitions as they come in, and this was one of forty-four fragments that were sold to the library by the executors of an estate on Wednesday, 23 February 1876. The estate was that of the German scholar Constantin Tischendorf.

Constantin Tischendorf had, twenty years earlier, made the greatest manuscript discovery of all time. This was not the Archimedes Palimpsest but the earliest surviving complete copy of the New Testament, together with substantial portions of the Old Testament in Greek, now known as the Codex Sinaiticus. It was written between about AD 330 and 350, and it may be one of the original fifty copies of the scriptures commissioned by the Roman Emperor Constantine after his conversion to Christianity. It was written in the type of majuscule script in which Isidore of Miletus would have written his texts. Tischendorf found it in the ancient and secluded monastery of St Catherine's, in the Sinai Desert. Tischendorf negotiated with the monks to borrow the codex and conveyed the manuscript to the Russian Tsar Alexander. The Tsar gave Tischendorf the title 'Von' before his surname, thereby making the son of a German physician a Russian nobleman, and paid the monks 9,000 roubles for the codex. Good deal.

Tischendorf was, among other things, a very great biblical scholar. He had no difficulty in recognising the importance of the Codex

Sinaiticus. But why was he in possession of a folio from the Palimpsest, and how on earth did he get hold of it? Actually, he nearly tells us himself. In 1846 he published a book entitled *Travels in the East.* In it he recounts a visit to the Metochion (Dependency) of the Jerusalem Holy Sepulchre in Constantinople, where he found nothing of particular interest, except for a palimpsest containing mathematics. We know the Palimpsest was at precisely this location in 1899 because Papadopoulos-Kerameus then catalogued it there. Clearly it was already in the Metochion in the 1840s, and clearly Tischendorf had come away from his visit with a folio torn from it.

Of course we do not know how the manuscript moved from St Sabas back to Constantinople, and when John Dean and I had actually tried to visit the Metochion of the Holy Sepulchre, when we were in Constantinople, there was no one to ask. It was Easter, and all the monks had gone to Jerusalem, to their mother institution – the patriarchal Monastery of the Holy Sepulchre in Jerusalem. The manuscripts of St Sabas had been incorporated into the library of the Greek patriarchate early in the nineteenth century. It is not hard to imagine, therefore, the circumstances in which a useful prayer book ended up back in the city in which it had been made seven hundred years earlier.

Back from the Dead

The front page of the *New York Times* for Tuesday, 16 July 1907 records a sensational discovery: Professor Heiberg, from Copenhagen, had discovered a new Archimedes manuscript in Constantinople. A certain Professor Schöne had brought his attention to the description of a codex in the 1899 catalogue by Papadopoulos-Kerameus. Papadopoulos-Kerameus didn't have tenure and was paid by the page for his work. Perhaps this was why, when he catalogued manuscript number 355, he not only described the contents of the prayer book in detail but also transcribed a section of an erased text that had been written over. Heiberg recognised the transcribed erased text as the work of Archimedes. He first tried, through diplomatic channels, to have the manuscript sent to Copenhagen, but this failed. Therefore in the summer vacation of 1906 he travelled to Constantinople and met the librarian of the Metochion, a Mr Tsoukaladakis, who allowed him to study the manuscript. There he discovered the staggering truth: Heiberg had found a sleeper, containing the unread greatest thoughts of a mathematician of genius.

Heiberg published Archimedes' letter to Eratosthenes, the *Method*, in an academic journal called *Hermes*. Between 1910 and 1915 Heiberg completely re-edited the works of Archimedes to incorporate his readings from the Palimpsest. His edition is ultimately based on three codices: Codex A (now lost), which was number 612 in the Pope's library in 1311, Codex B (now lost), which was number 608, and Codex C (now found), which is the Archimedes Palimpsest.

These publications are the work of an extraordinary scholar, but they are also the work of a man limited by a number of factors. First, the physical constraints of the bound prayer book: as we will see, the scribes of the prayer book had constructed their manuscript in such a way that two or three lines in the middle of every folio of the original Archimedes manuscript were hidden from view, in the gutter. In such places, Heiberg simply had to guess what was written. Secondly, he had to work with the technology of his day; he did not even use ultraviolet light, which is now a standard procedure for people reading faint texts. Thirdly, he was limited by the intellectual framework within which he operated. Heiberg was a philologist. A philologist is a lover of language, not of drawings. He paid no attention to the diagrams in the codex. For his *Hermes* publication he had a mathematical colleague called Zeuthen reconstruct the diagrams from the Archimedes text. But as Reviel jumped up and down to tell me, ancient mathematicians didn't think in text; they thought in diagrams. The Palimpsest was the unique source for the diagrams that Archimedes drew in the sand in the third century BC and they had never been studied. Finally, Heiberg was only really interested in Archimedes. He did mention that there were other works in the Palimpsest, and he read just a few words of one of them, but he was totally unexcited by all the palimpsested pages except those that originally belonged to Codex C. Despite the work of the great Johan Ludvig Heiberg, there was still a great deal to be learned from the Archimedes Palimpsest.

So there was a lot of work yet to be done on the Palimpsest, and scholars throughout the twentieth century knew it. But they couldn't go and see it. The Archimedes Palimpsest had disappeared.

Lost in Paris

By 1938 the Metochion's manuscripts had all been moved to the National Library of Greece, in Athens. It was done under the noses of the Turkish authorities, who had specifically forbidden such exports. Certainly this was safer for the books than to have stayed at the Metochion, because life there had become very unpleasant.

At the end of the First World War an English and French military presence in Constantinople supported the Sultan of a crippled Turkish Empire – the Old Man of Europe. Mustafa Kemal – later Ataturk – left the capital and rallied Turkish nationalists to found the modern state of Turkey. By 1923 the Allies and the Sultan had been ousted from Constantinople. In the process, Ataturk had also roundly defeated the Greeks, who had rashly invaded Turkey in 1921. In an early example of ethnic cleansing, hundreds of thousands of Greeks living in Turkey were forcibly transferred to Greece. Then, in 1925, Ataturk abolished religious orders and hanged the Greek Patriarch of Constantinople.

It was in this atmosphere that the books in the Metochion were surreptitiously moved to Athens. There are no records of how it was done; but it was necessarily done very quietly. And this veil of silence that surrounded the Metochion manuscripts in the twenties and thirties must have been just too tempting for someone. Because the

Palimpsest was one of a number of spectacular manuscripts that never made it to Athens.

These manuscripts are now in various institutions, including the University of Chicago, the Cleveland Museum of Art, the Bibliothèque Nationale in France, Duke University and, lo and behold, the Walters Art Museum in Baltimore. Henry Walters bought one as well – a beautiful Gospel book, now Manuscript W.529. The Palimpsest was not nearly as beautiful as these books, but something was done about that. In one very striking respect the book looks very different from the one that Heiberg saw. Those four painted pages that I thought were charming when I first looked at the book were not there when Heiberg studied it. The catalogue says:

> Four leaves, all now detached, are illuminated with full-page portraits, presumably intended to represent the Evangelists. Some of the colors look strangely modern ... Neither Heiberg nor Papadopoulos-Kerameus in his description refers to them, so they must be relatively recent, presumably a misguided attempt at the Metochion to embellish the manuscript and enhance its value in the eyes of a prospective purchaser. The pictures have been painted over both upper and lower scripts. All four leaves are listed by Heiberg as containing text by Archimedes ...

In other words, these pictures were forgeries. Gold, lead, copper, barium, zinc and a whole host of other elements had been plastered over the flesh and iron that encoded the unique text of the letter that Archimedes had sent to Eratosthenes! As if the scribe of the prayer book had not done enough to obliterate Archimedes, his greedy successors had poured insult on to injury and painted over his corpse.

The auction catalogue merely says that the book left the Metochion and ended up in a private collection in France. However, the court case over the rightful ownership of the manuscript instigated by the Greek patriarchate meant that further explanation had to be given, and it resulted in the documents that Mr B sent to me after he left the Palimpsest in my care. The most revealing of them is the sworn

The Archimedes Palimpsest, as it arrived at the Walters Art Museum on 19 January 1999.

The Palimpsest open. The right-hand page contains the unique text of Archimedes' *Method*, proposition 14. All you can see is the prayer book text. The indent to the page on the bottom right is the armpit of the goat from which the page was made.

The Euryalus fortress overlooks the city of Syracuse, Sicily. Its ramparts remain imposing more than 2,200 years after the city was stormed by the Romans, and Archimedes killed, in 212 BC.

Built in AD 537, Hagia Sophia dominates the skyline of Constantinople. It was designed in part by Isidore of Miletus, who was responsible for an edition of Archimedes' works in the sixth century.

(*Facing page*) A medieval scribe. This picture of St Luke was painted in the Byzantine Empire in the thirteenth century. St Luke writes on a piece of parchment with a reed pen. On a lectern in front of him is the book he is copying from, written in majuscules. Resting on the table are further implements of his trade, and in the cupboard a vessel containing ink.

Ο Α ΛΟΥΚΑC

Constantinople, present-day Istanbul, as viewed from the Galata Tower, with the Golden Horn in the foreground, and Hagia Sophia on the skyline. It was this view that faced the crusaders in April 1204, when they sacked the city.

The Monastery of St Sabas in the Holy Land. This was the resting place for the Archimedes manuscript from at least the sixteenth century until the early nineteenth.

This leaf was taken from the Archimedes Palimpsest by Constantine Tischendorf in the early 1840s when the book was at the Metochion of the Holy Sepulchre in Constantinople. Identified by Nigel Wilson in 1968, it fits between folios 2 and 3 of the Palimpsest. It is now in Cambridge University Library.

Abigail Quandt, Senior Conservator of Manuscripts and Rare Books at the Walters Art Museum. The conservation of the Palimpsest rested almost entirely on her shoulders.

Abigail performs brain surgery. Here she mends a damaged leaf of the Archimedes Palimpsest.

It took four years to disbind the Archimedes Palimpsest. This is a rare action shot.

Heiberg's photograph of folio 57r of the Archimedes Palimpsest, which contains part of the introduction to Archimedes' *Method*.

An illustration in H. Omont's 1929 publication of Greek manuscripts in the Bibliothèque Nationale.

Folio 57r of the Archimedes Palimpsest as it is now. The text is covered with a forgery, painted after 1938. The image of the scribe was traced on a one-to-one scale from the picture in the Omont publication.

An X-ray fluorescence image of folio 57r, taken at SLAC, to reveal the texts beneath the forgery.

A detail of the Archimedes Palimpsest before it was disbound. Note how the lower half of the picture contains a very faint diagram that disappears into the gutter.

(Left) The Palimpsest in normal light. It is very difficult to discern any undertext. *(Right)* An early experiment, this is a highly processed image of the same area. It seems to show diagrams and Archimedes text. Despite appearances, it did not help the scholars very much.

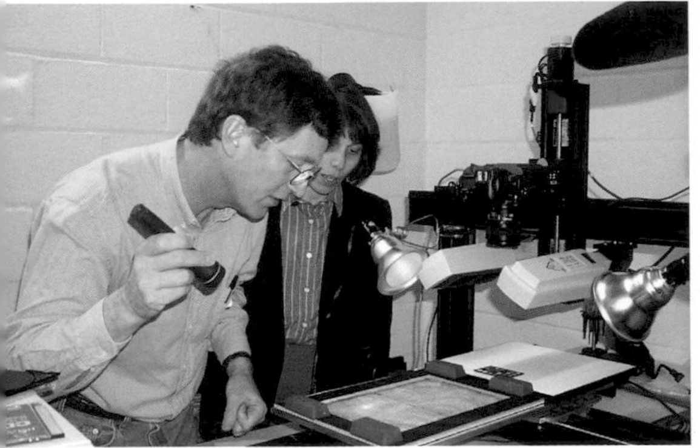

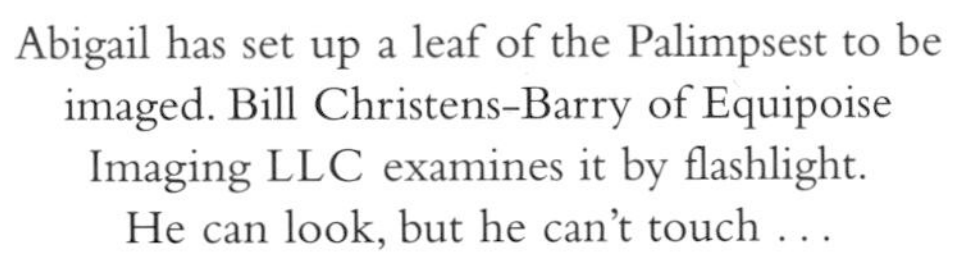

Abigail has set up a leaf of the Palimpsest to be imaged. Bill Christens-Barry of Equipoise Imaging LLC examines it by flashlight. He can look, but he can't touch . . .

Roger Easton, Professor of Imaging Science at the Rochester Institute of Technology inspects the optical imaging system.

Bill Christens-Barry demonstrates the narrow band imaging system that he designed.

Keith Knox, Chief Scientist at the Boeing Corporation, Maui. He invented the algorithm by which so much of the text was revealed. Here he is acting in his capacity as 'lights'.

affidavit from someone called Robert Guersan. Robert Guersan was the son of Anne Guersan, who owned the manuscript before the sale. He believed that his grandfather, Anne Guersan's father, Marie Louis Sirieix, had acquired the Palimpsest in the 1920s and had kept it in his house in Paris.

Sirieix had served in Greece in the First World War and travelled in Greece and Turkey in the early 1920s. This was presumably when he had laid his hands on the manuscript. He had lived in Paris, served with distinction in the French Resistance in the Second World War and left for the South of France in 1947. It was then that he had left the Palimpsest in the care of his daughter, who had taken over his apartment. He died in 1956.

In the sixties Anne Guersan began to look into the book she had inherited. She sought advice from Professor Bollack, a neighbour in Paris, and Professor Wasserstein, in Leicester. By 1970 at the latest, when she left a few detached leaves of the codex with Father Joseph Paramelle at the Institut du Recherche et d'Histoire des Textes of the Centre Nationale de la Recherche Scientifique, in Paris, she knew what she had. In 1971 she took it to the Etablissement Mallet 'to remove fungus stains from a few of its pages and otherwise to preserve its condition'. Then she set about selling it. In the 1970s a short brochure was produced and it was discreetly offered for private sale to a number of individuals and institutions. All declined. Anne Guersan finally turned to Felix de Marez Oyens, of the Manuscripts Department at Christie's.

The Palimpsest arrived on my desk on 19 January 1999, before the legal issues raised at the time of its sale were resolved. While John Dean and I were on our jaunt around the Mediterranean, Christie's and the patriarchate were still thrashing things out in court. We had more fun than they did. They did not disagree over the facts. The case turned on the interpretation of law, and Judge Kimba Wood ruled in favour of Christie's. In French law, which she judged applied in this case, as long as Anne Guersan had owned the codex publicly, peacefully, continuously and unambiguously for thirty years, she had the right to sell it. The burden of proof rested with the patriarchate's lawyer to demonstrate that she had not owned it in these circumstances, and the patriarchate's lawyer did not come up with such evidence. Judge Wood also noted that, should New York law be deemed to apply, she would still rule in favour of Christie's, but on a different principle – the principle of laches. Generally, the principle of laches is applied where it is clear that a plaintiff unreasonably delayed in initiating an action and a defendant was unfairly prejudiced by the delay. Judge Wood must have thought that bringing an action the night before the auction was an unreasonable delay. The case was finally dismissed only on the Wednesday, 18 August, by which time the exhibition was already open at the Walters.

I had learned a lot in five months. Sure, there were plenty of holes in my story. But I knew enough to think that it was a tragic one. I did not know the name of the fool who had obliterated the Archimedes text, and I did not know when, why or where he did this. But still, I had enough for a show, and I could give it a happy ending by promising to reveal the erased texts despite all that had happened to the manuscript. 'Eureka: The Archimedes Palimpsest' opened on Sunday, 20 June 1999 and travelled to the Field Museum in Chicago in the fall. The Palimpsest was opened to a folio on which visitors could just barely make out the diagram that accompanied proposition 1 of Archimedes' letter to Eratosthenes.

The exhibition started with John Dean's movie. The movie tells a strange story: ideas begin in the head of a man living on a triangle in the middle of the Mediterranean in the third century BC. These ideas are uniquely preserved today on a manuscript written in Constantinople twelve hundred years later. They survive the rise and fall of empires, the sacking of cities and the many changes in writing technology. And even though these ideas are scraped off and written over, they are still there. It is an astonishing journey. The letter beginning 'Archimedes to Eratosthenes, Greetings', starts right at the top of folio 46r column 2 of Codex C, and there alone. Delightfully, you can see the decoration marking the beginning of the letter and the name Archimedes quite clearly, before the column gets swallowed up by the text of the prayer book.

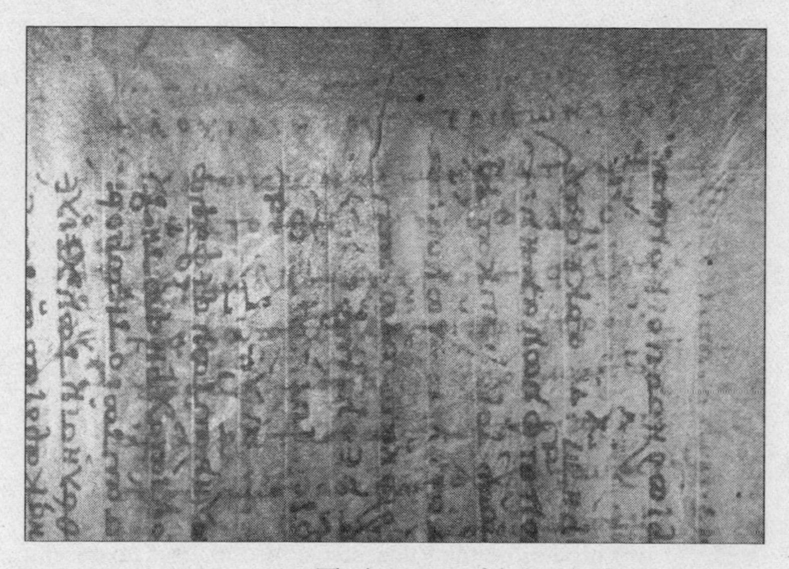

FIGURE 5.2 *The beginning of the* Method

6

Archimedes' *Method*, 1999 or The Making of Science

I was there, in June 1999. What a sensation that was, to see the Palimpsest open to the first diagram of the *Method*! I had always dreamed of seeing this one. That it was partially hidden from sight, disappearing into the gutter, only added to its mystery. I saw all those visitors coming in to gape at this modest-looking page, and I knew that they were looking at the only surviving evidence for Archimedes' greatest achievement.

The *Method* survives on the Palimpsest alone – there is no trace of it elsewhere inside other Greek manuscripts, no Arabic version, no Latin translation. The Palimpsest is the only physical object in the universe to bear witness to this achievement of Archimedes – which is unique not only among the Archimedean works but also among all other mathematics produced prior to the sixteenth century. Back in June 1999 we already knew – thanks to Heiberg's transcription – that Archimedes here came closest to the modern calculus. We also knew that Archimedes came closest to revealing his method, by which physics and mathematics can be brought together. These are the two keys to the science of Archimedes: the calculus, i.e. the mathematics of infinity, and the application of mathematics to physics. Mathematics, infinity, physics: this triple combination is all present in the *Method*. We shall see how – by following two great mathematical proofs.

The first proof, an example of the application of mathematics to the physical world, is Archimedes' discovery of the centre of gravity of a triangle. It is a result found outside the *Method*, but it is crucial for an understanding of how the *Method* works. The second proof is an example of the triple combination: mathematics, physics, infinity. It is the first proposition of the *Method*, where Archimedes finds the area of a parabolic segment. This brings us to the very height of Archimedes' achievement, collecting along the way the tool kit required for the making of modern science.

The Centre of Gravity

The first tool we need for modern science is the minuscule size of a point, and it is of vast significance. Science can not be made without it. This is the centre of gravity.

Let us put ourselves in the place of a physicist – say, in Newton's place. We wish to consider the motions of heavenly bodies under the influence of gravity. There is a fundamental problem: stars and moons are large bodies; they possess *structure*. Let's put this with the following example: the dark side of the Moon is further away from the Earth during a full moon than is the bright side of the Moon. And so the Earth's gravity acts less powerfully (being further away) on the dark side than on the bright side. If we wish to be precise, we can say that each point of the Moon has a slightly different gravity acting on it. There are infinitely many points in the Earth each exercising gravity, slightly differently, on infinitely many points in the Moon. How many combinations of gravities? Infinity times infinity. The problem has the complexity of infinity multiplied by infinity!

Yet Newton was capable of calculating his gravities. He dealt with the motions of heavenly bodies on the assumption that each of them acts *as a single point*. In Newtonian physics, for most purposes, the Earth is a single point, the Moon is a single point. There is only one point – the Earth – exercising gravity on only one point – the Moon. Such points are the *centres of gravity*. That is, we look for the point which is the 'average' of the weight or gravity of the Earth, and the point which is the 'average' of the weight or gravity of the Moon,

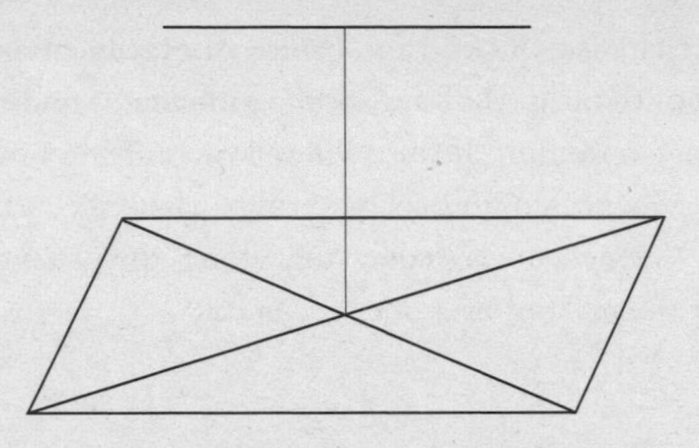

FIGURE 6.1 *Hanging a parallelogram*

and then we treat the Earth and the Moon as if they were all concentrated in those single points. It can be proven mathematically that, for most calculations, once we find the centre of gravity, then we can calculate with a single point instead of with the entire object. No physics can exist without the centre of gravity. And it is, once again, an invention of Archimedes.

The idea of 'centre of gravity' is best understood with a planar, two dimensional object. Let us take a circle. We wish to balance it; we wish to hang it from the ceiling so that it remains stationary. Where do we tie the thread? This is the easiest case: clearly, we tie the thread to *the centre of the circle.* Anywhere else, away from the geometrical centre – and the circle will collapse. To have it stationary, the circle must be hung precisely from its geometrical centre. In this easiest case, then, geometrical centre and centre of gravity coincide.

A square also hangs stationary when the thread is tied to its exact middle. The same is true for all parallelograms, as a moment's reflection will show. Take the point where the two diagonals meet, and you find the centre of gravity of a parallelogram (see fig. 6.1). But the question begins to be truly difficult once we get to more complex objects. The key to them all is the triangle. The triangle no longer has an obvious centre – the way a circle, a square or even a parallelogram has. But once we find the centre of gravity of the triangle, we can find the centres of gravity of all other rectilinear objects. As we have seen already, all rectilinear objects can be measured by dividing them into triangles. To find the centre of gravity of any rectilinear object, then, we need first to crack the problem of finding the centre of gravity of a triangle. The rest will follow easily.

The following, then, is the key to the science of centres of gravity: we cut a paper triangle and hang it from the ceiling. How do we hang it so that it remains stationary? How do we go about answering this question? – How does one pursue the science of centres of gravity?

You might wish perhaps, at this point, to conduct an experiment. You might wish to take several paper triangles and hang them from the ceiling from various points, in this way finding out where the centre of gravity happens to be. This approach makes sense: after all, you can't tell how the world behaves without checking it out for yourself. Your mind cannot dictate to the world how it should behave and so, purely through thought, you're not going to find out how objects hung from the ceiling are going to behave. Science is about hard evidence, not about pure speculation.

Not quite: much of the time science *is* about pure speculation. Archimedes invents the concept of the centre of gravity, and then finds this centre without ever conducting an experiment, doing it all *in his head*.

Let us look at the process of finding the centre of gravity of a triangle. It is worth our while following this in detail: we shall now see Archimedes' mind in action. Here is the already advanced, thirteenth proposition of Archimedes' book *On Balancing Planes*.

PROOF ONE: HOW TO BALANCE A TRIANGLE, OR MIND OVER MATTER

As you recall, the language Archimedes uses for his science is beautifully spare. For this reason it is also a very difficult language to read, whether in the original Greek or in translation. Let me explain, then, in my own words but closely following Archimedes' own line of thought, how Archimedes balances a triangle. As usual, this involves some twists and turns.

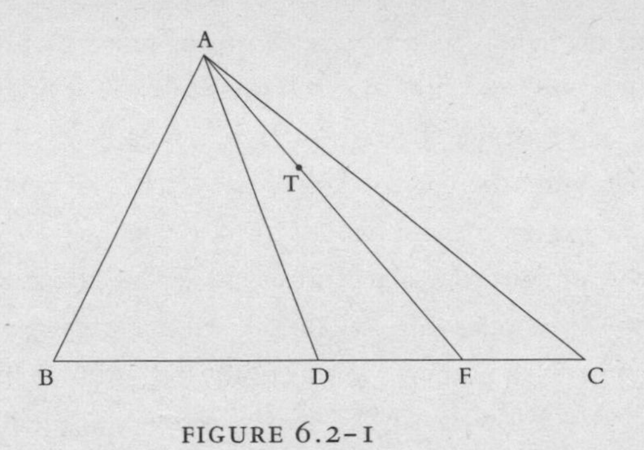

FIGURE 6.2-1

In figure 6.2-1 we take the triangle ABC, which we shall ultimately balance. We shall find the centre of gravity – the point from which we attach a thread so as to keep the triangle stationary. The line BC is divided into two at D (i.e. BD = DC). Thus the line AD is what is called a median in the triangle. Archimedes is going to prove that THE CENTRE OF GRAVITY OF A TRIANGLE MUST FALL SOMEWHERE ON A MEDIAN LINE. This is not yet finding the exact point; this is merely finding a line where this point lies. But bear with Archimedes: in geometry, one needs patience.

First of all, a piece of logical ingenuity: we are going to assume the opposite of what we want to prove. We are therefore going to assume that the centre of gravity does *not* fall on the line AD. In other words, we are going to assume that the centre of gravity falls on some other line, such as AF. Let us assume, then, that the centre of gravity is the point T falling on the line AF. This assumption will lead to an absurdity and therefore we will know that we were wrong, i.e. we will know that the centre does, after all, fall on the median line. As we have seen already, this is a logical technique greatly beloved by Archimedes, known as 'indirect proof'.

So, initially, we assume that the centre of gravity does not fall on the line AD but on some other point, T.

Now (see fig. 6.2-2) we introduce another complex piece of geometrical ingenuity. We add the points E and Z. E divides the line AB in two (so that AE = EB), Z divides the line AC in two (so that

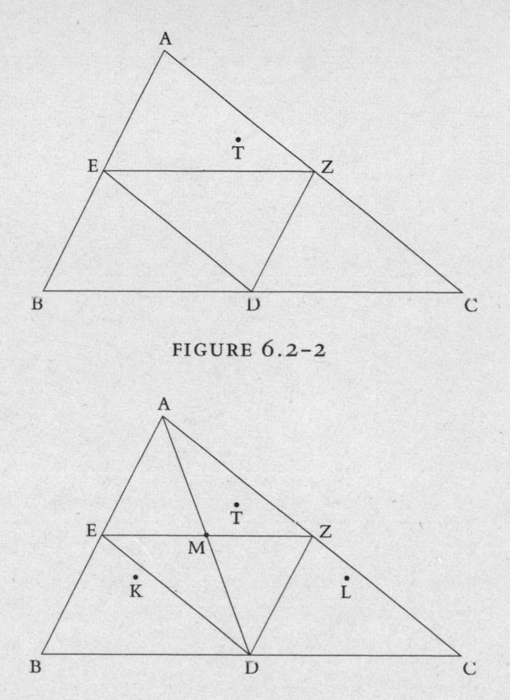

FIGURE 6.2-2

FIGURE 6.2-3

AZ = ZC). We connect the three points D, E, Z. Now inside the original, big triangle ABC we have four small triangles. If you were a Greek mathematician, it would not be difficult for you to prove the following nice fact: ALL FOUR SMALL TRIANGLES ARE SIMILAR TO THE BIG TRIANGLE, AND THEY ARE EQUAL TO EACH OTHER. Now, similar triangles are identical to each other in everything except size. Remember that we have assumed that T is the centre of gravity in the big triangle. So the centres of gravity of the smaller triangles will have to be similarly situated. Let us trace those centres of gravity in two of the smaller triangles. Now let us move on to figure 6.2-3.

These centres of gravity in the smaller triangles are to be the points L and K – L being the centre of gravity in the bottom-right triangle, K being the centre of gravity of the bottom-left triangle. What about the two remaining small triangles? They, in

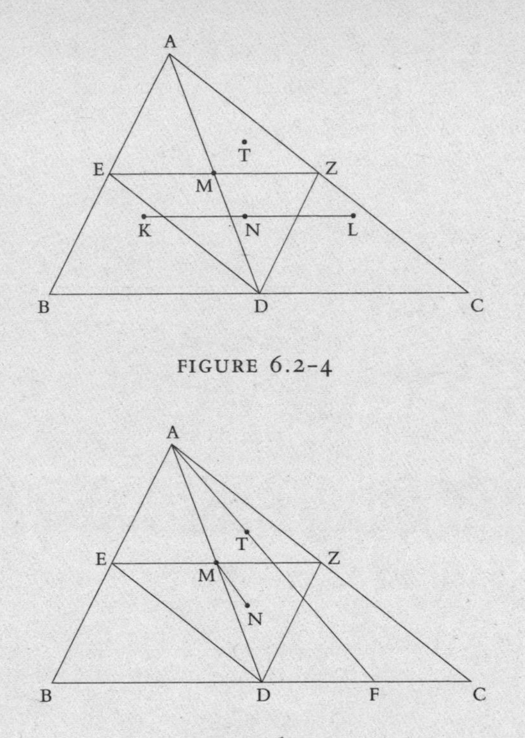

FIGURE 6.2–4

FIGURE 6.2–5

fact, taken together, constitute a parallelogram, and so simple considerations of symmetry show that their combined centre of gravity must lie at the point where the two diagonals of the parallelogram meet – the point M.

Now (see fig. 6.2–4) let us make the line KL. If we consider the two small triangles – the one at the bottom right and the one at the bottom left – as a single geometrical object, it is clear where their combined centre of gravity must lie. It must lie on the line connecting their respective centres of gravity, at its exact middle. That is, the centre of gravity of the two small triangles must lie at the exact middle of the line KL. Call this middle point N.

We are now ready (see fig. 6.2–5) to conclude our proof. We make the lines AT and MN. Now, M is the centre of gravity of two of the triangles, N is the centre of gravity of the remaining two. The combined centre of gravity of all four triangles, then – that is, the centre of gravity of the big triangle – must therefore fall exactly at the middle of the line MN. In this diagram we can clearly see that this is not where the point T lies, but this actually would be a bad argument to follow and a classic example of why one should not rely on diagrams too much. The question is this: how do we know that the point T can never lie on the line MN?

This is how. In any triangle, for the point T to lie on the line MN, the two lines MN, AF must intersect at some point (indeed, they must intersect at the point T!).

And they can't. It would be an easy task for Archimedes to show that *the lines AT, MN must always be parallel*. Therefore *they can never intersect*. We have asked the point T to lie on the line MN, and by doing this *have required two parallel lines to cut each other*! – and this must be wrong. No matter where I take my initial point T, as long as it is on a line such as AF which is not the median line AD, I shall always derive the same absurdity of two parallel lines being required to cut each other. So I know that the true position of the centre of gravity of any triangle is on its median line.

In any triangle there are, of course, not one but three median lines. It is proved that, when we draw all three median lines to a triangle – any triangle – they meet at exactly one point. In figure 6.2-6 we may see this as the triangle ABC, its sides bisected by the median lines AD, BZ, CE. All three lines, AD, BZ, CE, meet each other at the point X. This point X lies at an exactly defined position: it is one-third the way along the median line. DX is one third of AD, ZX is one third of BZ, EX is one third of EC. And this is where the centre of gravity must lie.

So Archimedes could suggest to you the following experiment. Take a paper triangle. Draw a median line. Find the point one-third of the way along that median line. Attach a thread to this point and hang it from the ceiling. The triangle is going to remain fixed and stationary. How does Archimedes know this? Oh, that's easy,

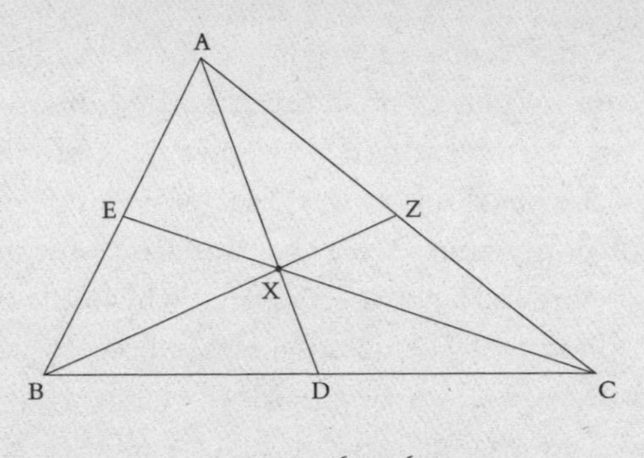

FIGURE 6.2-6

Archimedes explains. This is because lines, divided in two, give rise to four equal and similar triangles. This is because a certain line happens to be parallel to another. This is because of geometry. Follow logic, and you see for yourself. We turn away, in disbelief; but Archimedes is right.

The products of pure thought, which at first sight have nothing at all to do with each other or with the physical world, are brought together – and before you know it, this pure speculation binds the physical universe and forces it to behave in a particular fashion. I emphasise: no experiments whatsoever were required to find this out. Mind rules over matter – because, ultimately, even brute matter must follow logic.

This is rather like the magician telling us – without even looking – about the contents of our wallets. Archimedes has told us – without even looking – how the world must behave, where a triangle must balance.

Follow this a bit further. We start at Syracuse in the third century BC, and all we can do is hang a triangle from the ceiling. But follow this line long enough and you will be finally able, by the twentieth century, to launch a rocket to the Moon and to explode an atomic bomb. All the way down it's the same principle: you apply your power of reasoning to the universe, and the universe must follow logic. This is the principle discovered by Archimedes. This is science in action.

The Law of the Balance

Then there is another, complementary act of magic. Following the magic of mind-over-matter, of pure mathematics discovering a physical fact, comes another act of magic, no less spectacular: matter-over-mind, physics discovering a mathematical fact. This is done in the *Method*. Most historians of mathematics consider this the most amazing act performed by Archimedes. Besides being a piece of physics-over-mathematics, it also brings in infinity in a puzzling, strange way. In the next few pages, we shall follow all of this.

We need tools for this act. The first we have already: the centre of gravity of a triangle. The other is another physical fact, proved mathematically by Archimedes in the treatise *On Balancing Planes*. It is called the Law of the Balance, which we have already mentioned. It may equally be called the Law of the Lever: while these two machines do different things, they work by exactly the same mathematical rule. Archimedes relies on the balance for his measurements in the *Method*; but he was equally familiar with the lever and the law was most famously and succinctly expressed by him as follows: 'Give me a place to stand and I shall move the Earth.' That is: 'Give me a lever long enough, and I can move any object whatsoever.' Why is that? It is because of a principle of proportion. Let me now explain this, first with a balance.

We take any two objects, and put them on the balance. One arm of the balance has Object One, whose weight is, say, ten kilograms. The other arm of the balance has Object Two, whose weight is, say, two kilograms. The balances are of the moveable type, so that we can make each object nearer or further away from the fulcrum. The question is, at which distances will the objects balance. The answer is as follows: the ratio of the weights is 5:1, and therefore the ratio of the distances should be reciprocal, i.e. 1:5; the distance of the lighter object should be five times the distance of the heavier object – and then they balance. The rule is, weights balance when they are reciprocal to their distances.

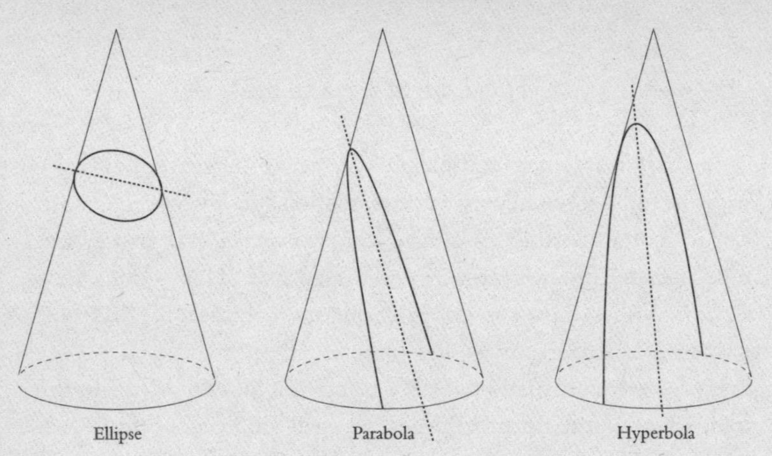

FIGURE 6.3 *The three conic sections. Take a cone and cut it in three ways: so that you cut from both sides – an ellipse; so that you cut parallel to one side – a parabola; and so that you cut moving away from one side – a hyperbola.*

If, instead of a balance, we have a lever, the same principle still holds: the object which is five times more distant is capable of exactly balancing an object five times heavier. Make it even more distant, and the lighter object will even move the heavier object. All of this Archimedes proved in *On Balancing Planes*, of course by pure thought: by standing in the realm of pure thought, Archimedes moved the Earth.

So I repeat: (a) the centre of gravity of a triangle is on the median line, one third along it; (b) objects balance each other when their distances are reciprocal to their weights. These are two facts about the physical world. With their aid, we shall measure the area of a segment of a parabola – that is, once again, find how a curved figure is equal to a rectilinear one (we have already seen Archimedes obtaining this result in one way; in the *Method* he obtains this in yet another, much more spectacular way) – which in itself is quite a surprise: who would think that triangles and balances would have anything to do with parabolas?

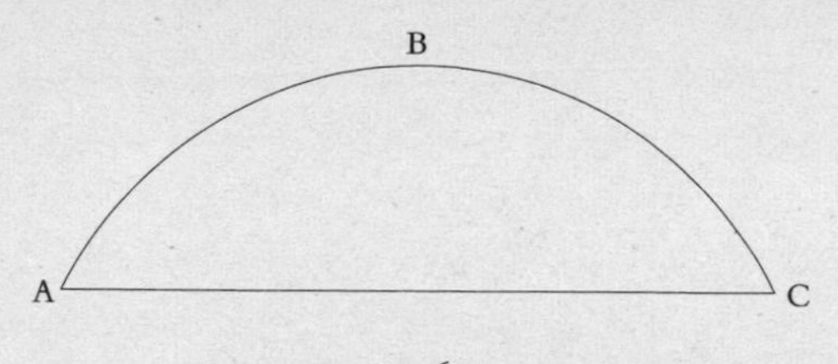

FIGURE 6.4–1

The Parabola

The very notion of a parabolic segment is very abstract. Parabolas belong to a family of curves invented by Greek mathematicians as an act of pure geometrical fancy, having no physical significance in mind. We take the surface of a cone, and we cut it by a plane. Depending on how we produce this cut, we may derive one of three sections: hyperbolas, parabolas or ellipses (see fig. 6.3). Circles, squares and triangles make sense: we more or less meet them in daily life. Not so hyperbolas, parabolas and ellipses. Their interest is mainly in the fact that – as it turns out – there are all sorts of nice geometrical proportions that arise with the combinations of conic sections.

Conic sections are best considered as toys invented by geometers to aid in their geometrical play. I keep returning to the irony of mathematics-over-physics, of how pure thought turns out to rule the physical universe, and this is one of the most remarkable ironies: the conic sections, which were invented as geometrical toys, turned out to be the curves defining motion in space. Electrons orbiting around the nucleus of an atom, a rocket launched to the Moon, a rock thrown by a catapult – all such motions obey the curves of conic sections. So that this study is, in fact, one of the major routes leading to modern science.

PROOF TWO: THE AREA OF A PARABOLIC SEGMENT, OR MATTER OVER MIND

We follow on this route, concentrating on the area of the parabolic segment (see fig. 6.4–1). By a 'parabolic segment' we mean the area

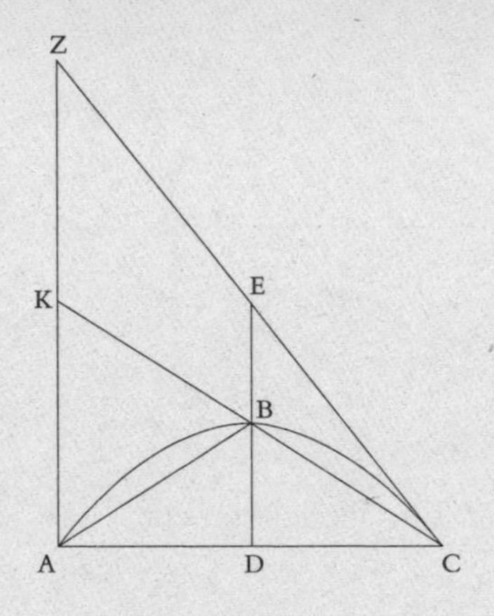

FIGURE 6.4–2

intercepted between a parabola and a straight line crossing through it, such as ABC (ABC is the parabola; AC is the straight line). You notice, of course, that a parabolic segment is a curvilinear object. This is the great mystery that constantly exercised Archimedes' mind: how to measure curvilinear objects; how to reduce them to rectilinear objects. Soon we shall see.

I move to the next figure (fig. 6.4–2) and note certain facts. First, each parabola possesses an axis of symmetry. In this case, it is the line BD, around which the parabola is 'the same', to the left and to the right.

To explain the following facts, we now need to add a few bits to the construction. We draw a tangent to the parabolic segment at the point C, namely the line CZ. We draw a line parallel to the axis, passing through the point A, namely the line AZ. You see that the tangent and the parallel meet at the point Z. All in all, we have enclosed the parabolic segment within a triangle: the segment ABC is enclosed within the triangle AZC. I also extend the line DB to reach the point E, and the line CB to reach the point K.

An interesting series of geometrical relations now ultimately depends upon the fact that the axis cuts exactly through the middle

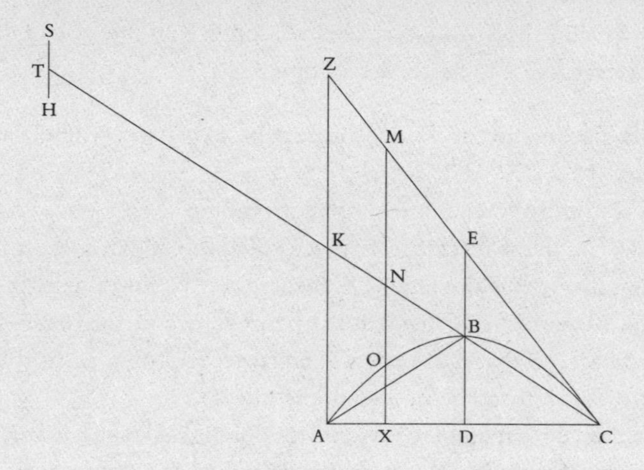

FIGURE 6.4-3

of the parabola (as well as on some other properties of the parabola). They are as follows:

- The point K is exactly at the middle of the line AZ.
- The point B is exactly at the middle of the line DE.
- The triangle AKC is exactly half the area of the triangle AZC.
- The point B is exactly at the middle of the line KC.
- The triangle ABC is exactly half the area of the triangle AKC.

Taken together, all of the above means, among other things, that:

- The great triangle AZC is four times the area of the small triangle ABC.

This is rather like the division of a triangle into smaller triangles that we saw with the previous proof, and it will be used by Archimedes later on.

Now I need to mention one of the funny facts about parabolas. We draw a line parallel to the axis of the parabola BD (see fig. 6.4-3) – any line; there are infinitely many such parallels, and we take one at random, say the line MX. So MX is parallel to BD. Here comes the funny fact (which, as it is typical, takes the form of a proportion):

- The line MX is to its smaller section OX as the base of the diameter AC is to its smaller section AX.

To the algebraically inclined, this can be expressed symbolically as follows: (MX:OX::AC:AX).

So we return to the line chosen at random, MX. We add a few more details in the diagram. First we extend the line from C, through B, onwards. It cuts the line MX at the point N, and it cuts the line ZA (as we have already seen) at the point K. We further extend it to the point T, so that KT becomes equal to KC, that is, so that the point K is exactly at the middle of the line TC.

We then do something very unorthodox. It will take us some time to see why we do this. But what we do is take the segment OX and, in our minds, we transport it to a new position SH, so that its middle point is now T, lying at the end of the line KC, extended. This is a thought experiment, then: we imagine a piece of geometrical line transposed. This is already sensational, because Archimedes has just moved a geometrical object – treating it as if it were physical, a piece of wood that one can carry about.

I now note a few consequences. First of all, I recall the original proportion, the funny result for parabolas:

- As MX is to OX, so is AC to AX.

Second, because the lines MX and ZA are parallel (this is how we have constructed the line MX), the ratio is preserved:

- As AC is to AX, so KC is to KN.

These are 'the same' ratios, simply sliding along the parallel lines. Combine the two above, and you can immediately see (eliminating the middle term, as it were) that:

- As MX is to OX, so KC is to KN.

The parallel line taken at random, MX, is to its smaller section, OX, not only as the base AC is to its smaller section AX; it is also as KC is to KN.

Further, remember that K is the exact middle point of TC, or TK = KC. So whatever is true of KC will also be true of TK. Therefore, it must also be true that:

- As MX is to OX, so TK is to KN.

The parallel line taken at random MX, to its smaller section OX, is the same ratio as TK to KN.

(Notice what Archimedes has achieved. His ratios until now have all been 'packed in', with a line relating to its own segment. This final ratio of TK to KN, however, unwraps the package and transforms the relation to one between two independent line segments touching at one point only. This will become useful later on.)

Finally, we may bring in another consideration. Whatever is true of OX must also be true of SH. This, after all, was our original thought experiment: to transpose OX so that it becomes SH. The two are identical. We noted above that the parallel line taken at random, MX, to its smaller section, OX, is the same ratio as TK to KN.

Now I exchange SH for OX – since the two are identical – to say the following:

- As MX is to SH, so TK is to KN.

The parallel line taken at random, MX, to its smaller section – now at SH – is the same as TK to KN.

This last proportion is the one we have been looking for. The magician is about to perform a trick. We have already engaged in one thought experiment, imagining the line OX as a physical line, transported to occupy the position SH. We now engage in another, much more radical thought experiment. No one has said anything remotely similar to this prior to Archimedes.

What we say now is that we imagine the lines MX and SH as lying on the arms of a balance, with its fulcrum at K. We now treat them as physical objects possessing weights – which will be a reflection of the objects' lengths. The two lines also possess centres of gravity, which will be, obviously, at their exact centres – that is, respectively, at N and T.

You see what we did: we just considered geometrical objects as if they were physical. I repeat: no one ever did this prior to Archimedes. Just as he invented the mathematical treatment of physics, he has also invented the physical treatment of pure mathematics.

Remember the previous result: 'MX is to SH as TK is to KN.' So what is the ratio of weight between MX and SH? It is the ratio of their lengths – the ratio of the line MX to the line SH. This, we have seen, is the same as the ratio of the line TK to the line KN – that is, the ratio of the lines is reciprocally the same as the ratio of their distances from the fulcrum.

Apply the Law of the Balance and derive the beautiful observation made by Archimedes: the two lines MX, SH will balance with K as their fulcrum.

Dizzying? Hold your breath: we now move on to another thought experiment, even more dizzying. Fresh from this trick, the magician now prepares yet another one.

The random line MX exactly balances its smaller section OX, around the fulcrum K, when that smaller segment is transposed so that its centre becomes T. But we chose the line MX randomly. No matter which other parallel line we choose, the same will hold true. The ratios will change, but they will remain respectively proportional.

In other words,

> Each parallel line inside the triangle AZC balances its respective section from the parabolic segment ABC (positioned at T), around the fulcrum K.

If you agree to that, you must agree to the following:

> All parallel lines, inside the triangle AZC, taken together, balance all their sections from the parabolic segment (positioned at T), taken together, around the fulcrum K.

Or, better still:

> The triangle AZC balances the parabolic segment ABC (positioned at T), around the fulcrum K.

How can it be otherwise? We slice the triangle and the parabolic segment, parallel line by parallel line, and each time we do the slicing we find the same balancing at the same fulcrum. So that when we take the entire triangle and the entire parabolic segment, they must obey the same law of the balance: the entire triangle and the entire parabolic segment must – just as each pair of their slices did – balance each other at exactly the same fulcrum.

So I repeat: the triangle as a whole balances the parabola as a whole, with K as the fulcrum.

We know where the centre of gravity of the transposed parabolic segment is: it is at the point T. This, after all, is our thought experiment: parallel line by parallel line, we have transposed the parabolic segment so that the centre of gravity of each line is T; if each line, taken separately, has its centre of gravity at T, then all taken together will do as well.

We can say then: the triangle, set at the position of the diagram, balances the parabolic segment, with the centre of gravity of the parabolic segment at T and the fulcrum at K.

What about the centre of gravity of the triangle? Well, we worked very hard on this question some few pages back. The centre of gravity of the triangle is at the point one third the way along the median line – that is, at the point one third of KC.

But one third of KC is also one third of KT – that is, the distance of the centre of gravity of the triangle from the fulcrum K is one third the distance of the centre of weight of the parabolic segment.

The parabolic segment is three times as far from the fulcrum as is the triangle; therefore the triangle must be three times the weight of the parabolic segment; therefore the area of the triangle must be three times the area of the parabolic segment.

We can make this result even more elegant. Consider the triangle

ABC, which, as we recall, is exactly one-fourth the triangle AZC. In other words, the parabolic segment ABC is four-thirds the triangle ABC.

Put simply: a parabolic segment is four-thirds the triangle it encloses.

This was a moment of magic. Consider that each treatise by Archimedes contains at least one such moment of magic and you begin to see the measure of the man. In the *Method*, each proposition is as magical. No wonder Heiberg was so excited in 1906.

Note the complex route leading to this magic. We take the thought experiment, of considering geometrical objects as physical ones. And then there is something further. We had a result for *pairs of slices*, pairs of random lines taken of the triangle and the parabolic segment. We then moved to *the triangle itself* and *the parabolic segment itself*, taken as wholes.

In other words, we took a proportion involving four lines, and turned it into a proportion involving infinitely many lines – all the infinitely many parallel lines constituting the triangle or the parabola.

Are we allowed to do that? This question, from now on – from Archimedes' time to our own – became the central question of mathematics. The *Method*, by bringing together mathematics, physics and infinity, already raised the most fundamental questions of science. It anticipated Newton's calculus – but it also anticipated the conceptual difficulties of that calculus.

How much did Archimedes know about infinity? In June 1999 we did not know. And this was the question on everyone's lips: what are we going to find, further, in the *Method* – if anything? We needed to look inside the Palimpsest and be able, finally, to read it. But in June 1999 Abigail had not yet unwrapped the book. The brain was still caged inside its box, as I was waiting, impatiently, for it to be freed.

7
The Critical Path

Conservators don't like being the centre of attention, but that's just where I had put Abigail Quandt: in the public eye and subject to its scrutiny. If you work on Leonardo's *Last Supper*, Michelangelo's *David*, or the unique witness to the thoughts of Archimedes, you'd better not slip up. Everybody tells you what you should be doing, but only you can do it. And no one had any idea of the problems that Abigail faced. They do now, but they didn't then. Hers was not only the critical path, as programme manager Mike Toth had characterised it; it was also the most important and the most onerous. Like Reviel, you are going to have to wait until you get more of the *Method*. This is Abigail's story.

You are probably thinking of Abigail as a book conservator, and that is what she is. But Abigail is not a normal book conservator. Most book conservators work with paper books; very few work on parchment manuscripts. There are good reasons for this. First of all, there are many more paper books in the world than there are parchment ones. Second, in general, paper books need conservation treatment much more often than parchment books. This is particularly true if they are printed on bad paper, with a high acidity. Such books are literally self-destructing in libraries across the globe as we speak. Many are the paper conservators who fight this battle. Parchment does not have this acid problem, and it is much tougher than paper. One essential difference between parchment and paper, however, is that parchment is much more sensitive to changes in temperature and humidity – it is skin, after all. If you lay a sheet of parchment over your sweaty hand it will quickly curl. Actually, it will curl into the shape it had on the back of the animal from which it came. With finely illuminated manuscripts, such as those at the Walters, this can have serious repercussions. The pigments in the illuminations do not change shape with the parchment as humidity changes and after a while the pigments flake off. Abigail had been working on parchment with this kind of problem for more than twenty years. She was a parchment expert, and very few people have her skills. This was why she was almost uniquely qualified to work on the Palimpsest.

Normally, the best thing to do with a historic object is absolutely nothing – which is what conservators do most of the time. Don't touch it; secure and monitor its environment. After all, a codex that has survived a thousand years is unlikely to degenerate much further if it is not handled and if it is not subject to pollutants or extremes of climate. In the past, even well-intentioned treatments have resulted in permanent damage and the loss of important historical evidence. In the nineteenth and early twentieth centuries many palimpsests in particular were wrecked by the treatment they received. Scholars routinely read palimpsests by applying chemicals to them. In 1919 English novelist and manuscript scholar M. R. James wrote that erased text could be

> revived by the dabbing (not painting) upon it of ammonium bisulphide, which, unlike the old-fashioned galls, does not stain the page. Dabbed on the surface with a soft paint-brush, and dried off at once with clean blotting paper, it makes the old record leap to light, sometimes with astonishing clearness, sometimes slowly, so that the letters cannot be read till next day. It is not always successful; it is of no use to apply it to writing in red, and its smell is overpowering, but it is the elixir of palaeographers.

There were other such elixirs. The most powerful was Gioberti's tincture: successively applied coats of hydrochloric acid and potassium cyanide. I'll just repeat that: successively applied coats of hydrochloric acid and potassium cyanide. Needless to say, ammonium bisulphide,